REGARDLESS OF WHAT YOU WERE TAUGHT TO BELIEVE...

THERE IS NOTHING WRONG WITH YOU
FOR TEENS

CHERI HUBER

Also by Cheri Huber

From Keep It Simple Books
The Key and the Name of the Key Is Willingness*
How You Do Anything Is How You Do Everything: A Workbook
There Is Nothing Wrong With You: Going Beyond Self-Hate, Rev. Ed.*
The Depression Book: Depression as an Opportunity for Spiritual Growth*
The Fear Book: Facing Fear Once and for All*
Be the Person You Want to Find: Relationship and Self-Discovery*
Nothing Happens Next: Responses to Questions about Meditation
Sex and Money...are dirty, aren't they? A Guided Journal
Suffering Is Optional: Three Keys to Freedom and Joy

From A Center for the Practice of Zen Buddhist Meditation
That Which You Are Seeking Is Causing You to Seek*
Time-Out for Parents: A Compassionate Approach to Parenting*
The Monastery Cookbook: Low-fat Vegetarian Recipes

From Hay House
How to Get from Where You Are to Where You Want to Be

From Present Perfect Books (Sara Jenkins, editor)
Trying to Be Human: Zen Talks from Cheri Huber*
Turning Toward Happiness: Conversations with a Zen Teacher and Her Students
Good Life: A Zen Precepts Retreat with Cheri Huber
Buddha Facing the Wall: Interviews with American Zen Monks
Sweet Zen: Dharma Talks with Cheri Huber

*Videotapes from Openings***
There Are No Secrets: Zen Meditation with Cheri Huber
Yoga for Meditators *with Christa Rypins*
Yoga for A Better Back *with Christa Rypins and Dr. John Sousa*
Yummy Yoga: Stress Relief for Hips, Back, and Neck *with Christa Rypins*

*Available as a book on tape from Keep It Simple
**Also available from Keep It Simple
Please see the order form at the end of this book.
All items except books on tape are available through your local bookstore.

Published by Keep It Simple Books
www.keepitsimplebooks.com
Printed in the United States of America

ISBN 0-9636255-9-4

Cover design by Mary Denkinger
Cover art by Alex Mill

Printed on recycled paper

For Ramada
and
for Walter
in gratitude

Acknowledgments

My deepest appreciation to Christa, Michael, Jen, Chris, Dave, Melinda, Faith, Ann, Mickey, Tricia, Phil, Cameron, Jan, Margaret, Nancy S., Mark, Nancy D., Jennifer, Erin, the monks, and all who have facilitated our <u>There</u> <u>Is</u> <u>Nothing</u> <u>Wrong</u> <u>With</u> <u>You</u> retreats.

Special acknowledgment to all who have participated in our retreats.

Introduction

In the years since publishing our best-selling <u>Regardless of What You Were Taught to Believe, There Is Nothing Wrong With You,</u> people have said to me periodically, "I wish I had read this growing up." "I wish I had known this in high school." Finally I heard what they were saying: Young people need this information. It's too late for those of us who "grew up" ten, twenty, thirty, or more years ago, but those of you who are young today are growing up just as alone, isolated, and confused as previous generations, and facing a more complex world.

As I started this project I knew I wanted to hear from a widely diverse cross section of teenagers: city/country, poor/wealthy, all ethnic and racial groups, boys and girls. The surveys I sent out were anonymous, yet based on what teens volunteered about themselves, I've come very close to that goal. Most respondents were fifteen- to eighteen-year-olds, most lived at home, all were still in school, a few were teen mothers.

In discussing the survey with friends, educators, social workers, and those folks whose fortunes brought them to the seat next to mine on an airplane, I heard an amazing range of concerns, fears, and hopes about the teens of today. Many expressed a belief that teens are very different from how they themselves were at that age. Teens are generally as united in their basic assumptions about and approaches to adults as adults are in their approach to teens. Of course, there are exceptions. Obviously there are adults who are extremely sensitive to the needs of teenagers. Unfortunately those people are often not the parents of teenagers. One woman who works with teen girls told me, "You don't need to worry about talking to teenagers all over the country, talk to one and you'll have all the information you need. They are unique individuals, but they all have the same problems." After reading responses from and talking to many young people, I think she was not far from the truth. Just as parents of teens are much more similar in their responses to parenting than not, their teenage children are much more similar in their view of school, friends, the world and themselves than not.

The difficulty that exists in the relationship between teens and adults comes to one thing: communication. The constant theme I heard in conversation after conversation was
--adults don't listen
--adults don't care who we are or what we think
--adults think lecturing is communicating
--adults don't understand us and don't want to
--adults don't care how we feel
--adults think we understand more than we understand
--adults think asking a question is "talking back"

Harsh criticism. Hard for adults to hear. But hear it adults must if we are going to have a hope of being anything other than what teens have already judged us to be. If adults can't hear these criticisms, if parents and teachers cannot be open to the possibility that we are closed-minded and don't know it, the assessment teens have made of adults will prove to be accurate. The truly horrible result of this chasm is that your generation will grow up to parent exactly as you were parented.

I think something else is possible, we have another choice, and your generation is the one that can make the difference.

In loving kindness,
Cheri

Table of Contents

You've been taught
that there is something wrong with you
and that you are imperfect,
but there isn't,
and you're not.

Surviving Childhood: Establishing A Strong, Early Foundation for Self-Hate

Unless you were raised by wolves, the chances are extremely good that as you were growing up, you heard at least a few of the following:

Don't do that . . . Stop that . . . Put that down . . . I told you not to do that . . . Why don't you ever listen . . . Wipe that look off your face . . . I'll give you something to cry about . . . Don't touch that . . . You shouldn't feel that way . . . You should have known better . . . Will you ever learn . . . You should be ashamed of yourself . . . Shame on you . . . I can't believe you did that . . . Don't ever let me see you do that again . . . See, that serves you right . . . I told you so . . . Are you ever going to get it . . . What were the last words out of my mouth . . . What were you thinking of . . . You ruin everything . . . You have no sense . . . You're nuts. The nurses must have dropped you on your head . . . Just once, do something right . . . I've sacrificed everything for you and what thanks do I get . . . I had great hopes for you . . . If I've told you once, I've told you a thousand times . . . Give you an inch, you take a mile . . . Anybody would know that . . . Don't talk back to me . . . You'll do as you are told . . . You're not funny . . . Who do you think you are . . . Why did you do it that way . . . You were born bad . . . You drive me crazy . . . You do that just to hurt me . . . I could skin you alive . . . What will the neighbors say . . . You do that to torture me . . . You're so mean . . . I could beat the daylights out of you . . . It's all your fault . . . You make me sick . . . You're trying to kill me . . . Now what's the matter with you, cry baby . . . Go to your room . . . You deserve it . . . Eat it because children are starving . . . Don't stick your lip out . . . If you cry, I'll slap you . . . Don't you ever think about anyone else . . . Get out of my sight . . . and on and on and on and on and on and on.

Somewhere along the line, you concluded that there was something wrong with you.

OF COURSE YOU DID!

WHAT ELSE COULD YOU CONCLUDE!?

IF THERE WERE NOTHING WRONG WITH YOU,

PEOPLE WOULDN'T
TREAT YOU THAT WAY!

THEY WOULDN'T SAY THOSE THINGS TO YOU!

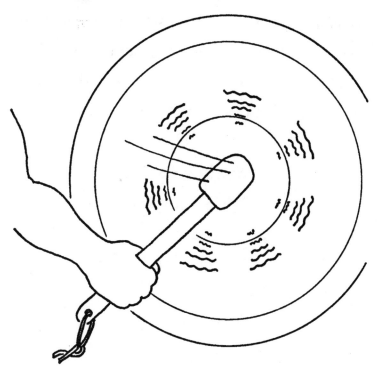

"Then why did they do that to me?"
Because it was done to them.
Because we do what we've been taught.
Because we do to children what was done to us.

In the same way we grow up speaking the language of our parents, if we're yelled at as children, we learn to yell at children; if we're hit as children, we learn to hit children; if we are ignored as children, we learn to ignore children.

Society calls this
"child rearing"
or
"socialization."

We call it
"sad."

The process of socialization teaches us:
- to assume there is something wrong with us
- to look for the flaws in ourselves
- to judge the "flaws" when we find them
- to hate ourselves for being the way we are
- to punish ourselves until we change

We've been taught that this is what good people do.

Socialization does not teach us:
- to love ourselves for our goodness
- to appreciate ourselves for who we are
- to trust ourselves
- to have confidence in our abilities
- to look to our heart for guidance.

We've been taught that this is "self-centered."

By the time "socialization" is complete, most of us hold an

UNSHAKABLE BELIEF

that our only hope of being good is to punish ourselves when we are bad.

We believe beyond doubt that without

PUNISHMENT

bad would win out over good.

This entire book
is based on the premise
that that is not true!

A Conversation with Teens:

CH: A lot of kids seem to feel that the world today is a lot different from the world their parents grew up in. Does that seem so to you?
A: It's not that different. They had all the same things, drugs, sex, and rock 'n' roll. But now there's AIDS.
CH: So, AIDS is scary to you?
Group: (Big chorus of) Yeah.
D: When my parents were being sexual as teens there was concern about reputation and pregnancy, and that was pretty much it. With us, there's AIDS.
B: Yeah, we get to have sex and maybe die. That's scary.

CH: What do you wish adults understood about people your age?
B: I think they understand, because they were our age and they wanted to do exactly what we want to do. But for some reason they don't want us to do what they did. Even though their

9

lives turned out fine, even though they have perfectly fine lives, they don't want us to follow them.

CH: So, do you feel like you know what happened with your parents, and they just won't cop to it?

Q: Sure. They say, "I did that but you shouldn't do it because it's bad. Even though I did it, you shouldn't do it. You should learn from my experience."

T: But we don't want to learn from someone else's experience. We want to have our own experience and learn from that. What happened to them doesn't mean anything to me. I want to find out for myself.

F: They think because they did something we're going to do it, too.

CH: So, adults keep bringing up the same stuff over and over and maybe you wouldn't even be thinking about it if they didn't keep bringing it up.

F: They keep accusing us of planning things that we're not even thinking about.

S: Sometimes they tell us too much. My parents have told me stuff I didn't want to hear like about where and when I was conceived and things they did when they were young. It's weird.

R: They don't want to hear about what I'm doing, they just start screaming, but they want to tell me stuff about what they did.

B: I think if you want advice you should ask for it instead of letting your parents give it to you all the time.

CH: Ok, so what's it like to talk to your parents?

X: It's funny. It's weird. I ask my mom something and she tells me the truth. I asked her when she lost her virginity and she told me when she was seventeen and that after that she couldn't stop having sex! I thought, omigod! I don't want to know that! She just kept telling me about it. It was not a pleasant conversation.

CH: Speaking of talking to parents, do you feel like your parents are interested in what you have to say?

Group: No, not particularly. It depends on the parent and the situation.

X: They're interested when you don't prove that they're wrong. If they're wrong, they're not going to cop to it.

R: And when I do something good, they just want to talk about something I did wrong.

CH: So, they're not real forthcoming with praise or support or encouragement.

R: (Laughter) No, they just want to yell at you for everything bad you do, nothing good.

B: They don't let you talk back. Their idea of a conversation is interrogation. They say something and you try to say something back and they don't want to hear it. They say, "We want to talk to you about this." But they don't want you to say anything to them about it.

V: They won't let you question them and they won't explain their reasons. They won't ever tell you why.

CH: So do you often find yourself in a place of not understanding why they're doing what they're doing or demanding what they're demanding?

Group: YES!

CH: So what you're saying is that adults, even though they say they want to talk to you, aren't interested in having a conversation. Adults don't realize what conversation is. There isn't much of the one person says something then the other person replies.

V: Yeah, they want to preach.

G: They think a conversation revolves around their opinion and nothing else.

CH: And they're assuming you understand a lot of things you really don't understand?

Group: Yeah.

V: Like when my mom wants to talk to me, she never wants to talk to me on a personal level. She calls me out of my room and asks me "who ate the peanut butter?" And she yells at me like it's my fault. I did eat the peanut butter. I'm the one in the house who likes peanut butter. She always yells at me when she talks to me.

It's always like whatever it is is my fault. I never know if she's accusing me of something or if that's just the way she talks to me. But when I want to talk to her about something important she's, like, okay, whatever. But when it's not serious and she wants to talk to me, she gets mad. I can't remember the last actual conversation I had with my mom.

CH: Is that what it feels like, that you're really different from your parents?

Group: Not really.

T: I'm apparently just like my mom. We all turn into our parents and its horrible!

To be continued...

Child is born. → Child learns to turn away from self toward other to get needs met. (stops trusting intuitive knowing)

↓

Need is not met; child believes it is because s/he is bad.

Child abandons self and decides to be perfect (be who others want) "I just won't need anything." "I shouldn't be afraid." "I'll do everything right."

↓

Child begins to develop survival behaviors. These behaviors are self-denying, self-preserving, self-destructive. (shuts down emotionally; eats to stuff feelings; etc.)

←

Individual uses self-hating behaviors to try to be a good person. (values others over self; denies self unnecessarily; uses ideals against self)

↑

Suffering

↑

Person tries everything to make conditioning work.

↑

Awareness work

↑

Person finds compassion and self-acceptance

↗

Child is reborn. ↗

15

My Survival System Is Killing Me!

<u>What</u> <u>happened</u> <u>to</u> <u>you</u>, not who you are, makes you angry, fearful, greedy, mean, anxious, etc.

<u>What</u> <u>happened</u> <u>to</u> <u>you</u>, not who you are, makes you do things that aren't good for you that you can't stop doing.

We learned behaviors when we were very young in order to survive. We were taught to hate those behaviors and to see them as signs of our badness. Yet we keep doing them because it's all we know how to do. And we hate ourselves for doing them.

THE TRAP:
    I believe I must be this way to survive.
    I believe this way of being is who I am.
For instance, as a little kid I cry when I don't get my way. I don't want to, but I can't stop.
    I hate myself for being this way.

RESULT:

    self-hate = survival (self-hate = who I am)
    survival = self-hate (who I am = self-hate)

I am the way I am.
I can't help the way I am.
I hate myself for being the way I am.

"I grew up with my mother. I wish she had talked more about sex and drugs. I know she didn't want me to do them, but she never talked about them. I'm going to talk with my kids about sex and drugs, teach them about the consequences of doing those things, and I'm going to listen to them when they want to talk. I'm not blaming my mother. I love her. I just wish she had talked to me more about sex and drugs before I found out for myself."

Suffering provides our identity, our sense of who we are, our "me-ness." Identity is maintained in struggle and dissatisfaction and in trying to fix what's wrong.

We try to fix what's "wrong" with us
and the attempt to fix something
that isn't broken
keeps us stuck believing
there is something wrong with us.

In other words, I believe I'm ugly so I spend all my time and energy trying not to be ugly, but all the things I do to try not to be ugly just make me feel ugly. The solution: I need to realize I'm not ugly, I just believe I'm ugly. Hint: It's often easier to see this with friends. Think of a friend who thinks they are stupid or fat or ugly and realize you don't see them that way. You can see that their perception of themselves is inaccurate. Same with you!

Suffering,
egocentricity,
fear,
self-hate,
illusion of separateness
misery

} SAME THING

So we are constantly looking for what is wrong,
constantly creating new crises so we can rise to
the occasion. To ego, that's survival. It is very
important that something be wrong so we can
continue to survive it. Back to the crying
example: I have to always have something in my
life that I'm upset about because crying when I
don't get my way is how I know myself, it's how
I know who I am, and being that way means I'm
surviving. It doesn't make sense, but I can
watch myself do it over and over again. Even if
someone tells me I could just stop, I can't. It's
embarrassing and humiliating, but still I cry when
I don't get what I want.

Self-Hate Is A Process

Self-hate is a "how" not a "what."

Examples:

If I'm a worrier, worrying is the "how," the process. The things I worry about are the "whats," the content. *

If I am judgmental, judging is the "how," the process. The things I judge are the "whats," the content.

* The content can seem so real that I don't recognize the process. "Exams are next week, of course I'm worried." "I haven't been asked to the prom. What if no one asks me?" "My best friend is drinking so much these days." It is easy to miss that the only thing these events have in common is my process of worry.

If I am caught in self-hate, self-hating is the "how," the process. The aspects of "me" that are being hated, such as my body, my personality, my looks--the list is endless--are the "whats," the content.

In other words, I am not hating myself; the learned <u>process</u> of self-hate is hating me.

And self-hate is autonomous. It has a life of its own, an endless tape loop of conditioning, creating and shaping the world in which I live.

The simplest example is that if self-hate is hating my body,

it doesn't matter what I do or what I look like, I will never meet self-hate's standard, which is the point. Self-hate is not hating me to help me meet a standard. No. It is a process of hating and hating is just what it does.

As long as it exists,
it will find something about me to hate.
That's how it maintains itself.

Self-hate tells me I'm too fat. I decide to lose weight. I struggle and starve myself, hearing voices in my head tell me to eat all the fattening things I love and want, but I don't and eventually I lose weight.

Then self-hate tells me I'm not thin enough, and besides, my weight is not why people don't like me. They don't like me because I say stupid stuff. So I make a plan to be really careful about what I say, memorize some jokes, learn all the current lingo...

Then self-hate tells me that what I say isn't the problem, the problem is how I dress. People don't like me because of how I dress. So I make a plan...

I have to get it that I am never going to meet standards that change every time I get close to them.

"I would like to be skinnier, less complicated, not as sexually driven. I wish I didn't say exactly what was on my mind, wish I wasn't so trusting, so gullible. I wish I could fall in love and stay there, be able to keep a stable relationship."

The process of self-hate is so much a part of
the average person that we don't recognize it.

We think we're just doing the things that will
ensure we'll be good.
It's normal, we say. Everybody does it.
Or should.
For example,
you call yourself stupid when you get bad grades
as if that will make you work harder. Or you
worry before exams, believing that you won't
study if you don't worry.

At a very early age we learn to punish
ourselves as a way to get love and acceptance.
Most people will die of old age still trying to "fix"
themselves in order to be the person they
"should be" so they will finally be loved and
accepted.

Parents don't seem to be caught in this trap,
but they are.

If you want to know what you were conditioned
to believe as a child, look at how you treat
yourself now.

Does that mean someone consciously, deliberately
treated you that way?

Perhaps not.

But you got the message anyway,

didn't you?

A Scam Self-Hate Loves to Run

It is confusing for someone to conclude that they aren't loved because there is something wrong with them.

"I want to fit in and be accepted, but there's something wrong with me. I need to fix that, even though I'm not really sure I know what it is or how to fix it. But I must keep trying anyway because I really want to be accepted."

This person who is trying to become acceptable spends much time, attention and energy trying to be good, earn approval, please others, and

BE PERFECT.

And then, when they find that trying to be good doesn't work, doesn't in fact get the approval and acceptance they want, all they know how to do is

TRY HARDER.

It's like being on a journey and being completely lost,

going in the wrong direction but making really good time.

And what we are left with is confusion. "I'm trapped and confused. What I'm doing isn't working, but I don't know what to do instead." Confusion is the result of attempting to cling to a conditioned belief (if I try harder I can make it work) in the face of what you are seeing to be true for you (this isn't working, I feel powerless, there must be another way). *

If you will continue to pay attention, the confusion will give way to clarity. If you can find the willingness to LOOK, AND TAKE A STAND AGAINST THE SCAM SELF-HATE HAS YOU CAUGHT IN, the confusion will give way to clarity.

And the clarity is compassion.

*It's always a good idea to go back and check out the original premise. The faulty premise in this case is that if you meet the endless, changing, nebulous list of conditioning's standards, you will be who you should be, you will be lovable, and you will be loved. The truth is that you can never "earn" love by making yourself be who you

think others want you to be. Who you are is
lovable. If you are who you really are, behind all
the ways you're trying to become, not listening
to the voices that put you down, call you names,
make you think you're not good enough, you will
enjoy who you are and other people will enjoy
you. Sounds crazy, but it's true. It's the kind
of thing you just have to prove to yourself.
Hint: You already know this because there are
people who know who you really are and love you
for who you are. Those people are called, "best
friends."

"I wish adults would stop judging us on
the fact that we're teens. They see
a teenager walking down the street
and automatically assume they're in
a gang or will do something bad to
them or their children. We're not all
bad and we're not all like the kids
who pull guns out at school and shoot
their classmates."

A word of explanation: Throughout this book we refer to "beating" as something we are conditioned to accept as a way to be sure we're who we should be.

Beatings can be anything from inflicting physical harm on oneself (cutting, burning, abusing alcohol, drugs, or food) to self-criticism or name-calling. If you pay close attention you will notice that hearing yourself called fat or lazy or stupid _feels_ like you just got beaten up.

We use the term beating to refer to any interaction with yourself that is unkind or punishing, however mild that unkindness or punishment might seem.

Some of the Forms Self-Hate Takes

SABOTAGE

You try to do something good for yourself or for someone else and somehow manage to make a mess of the whole thing. You keep doing the very things you didn't want to do and don't approve of, and you can't seem to stop yourself. It's a perfect system for self-hate because:

1) You have an idea of how you should be.
2) You don't live up to your ideal.
3) You can't figure out where you're going wrong.

TAKING BLAME BUT NOT CREDIT

If something goes well, it's a gift from God. If it goes badly, it's all your fault. And even if you do take a little credit for something, you don't get to feel good about it because you know you could have done better.

BLAMING OTHERS

Self-hating and "other" hating are the same thing. Whether you are hateful toward

others or hating yourself directly, it's self-hate--
you are always the recipient.

BEING SECRETIVE

You don't let other people know what's
going on inside you so that you can be in there
beating yourself with it, and no one can help you
out.

HOLDING GRUDGES

You review old hurts and injustices rather
than being present to yourself now.

NOT BEING ABLE TO RECEIVE

Gifts, compliments, help, favors, praise,
etc. are things you have difficulty allowing
yourself to have.

SEEING WHAT IS WRONG WITH EVERYTHING

Your habit is to find fault, criticize, judge
and compare. Remember, what is is all that is.
The alternate reality in which everything is
exactly as you think it should be exists only in

your mind, and it exists primarily to torture you. You're always comparing yourself to how you should be and your "failures" make you miserable.

TRYING TO BE DIFFERENT

Just being who you are, your "plain old self," isn't enough. You feel you have to maintain an image.

ATTEMPTING TO BE PERFECT

BEING ACCIDENT PRONE

Your attention is so often focused on some other time, person or thing that you injure yourself in the present. You don't feel you deserve your attention. Others are more important.

CONTINUING TO PUT YOURSELF IN ABUSIVE SITUATIONS

Even if you realize that you have this pattern, your fear and self-hate are too strong to let you break out of it. You don't know why you stay in situations that are hurtful to you, but you keep staying.

MAINTAINING AN UNCOMFORTABLE PHYSICAL POSITION

You hold your shoulders in a way that creates pain. You clench your teeth. You "sit small" on the bus so as not to intrude into anyone else's space. You continue to let people call you by a nickname you don't like because you don't want to draw attention to yourself.

MAINTAINING AN UNCOMFORTABLE MENTAL POSITION

Clinging to "shoulds": "I should be able to excel in all my classes." "I should be good at sports." "I shouldn't be so fat." "I should have more friends."

Some Voices and Gestures and Actions of Self-Hate

A word or gesture can conjure up a whole lifetime of negativity or defeat or unworthiness. When the memories and emotions tied to that word or gesture arise, it's like having a truckload of self-hate dumped on you.

"I can't believe you did that! What's the matter with you?"

"God, Cheryl!" (tone of disgust)

A shrug of the shoulders and the words "It doesn't matter." (signals total defeat)

A sinking feeling of "I've done something wrong," and a feeling of panic, "What's the right thing to do now to fix it?"

Buying anything for anyone else but never anything for myself.

Wanting to eat something and a voice saying, "Can't you ever say no to yourself?" and realizing that I say no to myself all the time about everything except food.

NO KINDNESS FOR ME   NO FUN   NO GOOD ATTITUDE

NO HAPPINESS   NO PROPER NUTRITION   NO ASKING FOR HELP

NO OPENNESS WITH ADULTS

NO BEING HONEST ABOUT HOW I FEEL

The Voices

By way of explanation--

In this book we refer often to "the voices inside your head" or similar phrases.

We aren't talking about a psychological disorder.

"Voices inside your head" refers to the nearly endless stream of thoughts we all experience, the constant flow of judgments, ideas, criticism, opinions that we tell ourselves day in and day out.

And we want to emphasize
that it is important
not to believe that these "voices"
have helpful information for you
about yourself!

We use the terms
" self-hate"
and
" egocentricity"
to mean the same thing.

So far in this book we have been defining
self-hate for you.

So,

what is egocentricity?
Egocentricity is the illusion of being a separate
self, separate from everything--ourselves, each
other, life, the universe. The illusion of
separation results from the process of social
conditioning.

Egocentricity is interested in one thing and one
thing only: SURVIVAL AT ANY COST.

It will SAY AND DO ANYTHING to remain in
control of your life.
It will come through any door.
It will stop at nothing.

Self-Hate has many voices.
Here are a few.

VOICE: Nothing subtle about it.
"You're disgusting. You make me sick."

VOICE: Sounds like normal, helpful, constructive criticism.
"It was stupid of me to have said that. I must watch what I say." (Children learn early to call themselves and others "stupid.")

VOICE: Sounds like self-discipline; helpful in keeping us on the "right track."
"I must finish this now even though I'm exhausted. I must not give in to these little self-indulgences. Who knows where it would stop."

VOICE: Sounds really, really true and helpful; the voice of clarity and wisdom.
You read a book that is meaningful for you, but every sentence is translated into "I should be

39

like that." This voice might start out sounding sincere but soon slides into accusation. "I've been doing it wrong all this time. What's wrong with me?" Another example: You are reading a book, quiet and comfortable, just relaxing. Then this voice says, "They're going to come home and you're going to be in trouble."

VOICE: Blaming
"I shouldn't have said that. I should have known better."

VOICE: Comparing
"He has a nicer car than I do, but I'm better looking than he is."

VOICE: Low-grade undercurrent of dissatisfaction
"I don't really want to be here with these people, but I don't really want to be anywhere else either."

You can listen to the voices that say there is something wrong with you. It's actually very helpful to be aware of them.

Just don't believe them!

What could my parents have done differently? Not fought so much. Not gotten divorced. Not be hypocritical. Admit they were wrong. I'm never going to have kids. I don't want to do to kids what they did to me."

Most of what we have been

TAUGHT TO BELIEVE

we had to be

TAUGHT TO BELIEVE

BECAUSE

IT ISN'T TRUE!

This is why children have to be conditioned so heavily! WE WOULD NEVER HAVE REACHED THESE CONCLUSIONS ON OUR OWN!

If we could for a moment look at what we've been taught to believe with an unconditioned mind, we would see that not only is it not true,

it's absurd.

"So, where did all this self-hate come from?"

Socialization and Subpersonalities

We learn it as children, and we learn it whether we grow up in a loving family or not. The steps go pretty much like this.

1.

The child has a need.

EXAMPLE:
    The child is afraid.

2.

The need is rejected.

The need does not get met by the person who is looked to to meet it. The child is traumatized when this happens. The trauma/rejection becomes a subpersonality, a permanent aspect of this child's personality; a defense mechanism; a part of the child's survival system.

3.

The child comes up with a behavior as a means of survival in order to get the need met.

EXAMPLE:

If the child is afraid of the dark, she/he will get up and sneak a flashlight into the bed. This ability to devise a surreptitious plan to protect oneself becomes a subpersonality.

4.

The child simultaneously identifies with the authority figure who didn't meet the need ("They're right, I'm bad for being this way."), and identifies with the part of themselves who was rejected ("I'm afraid, and they don't love me because I'm afraid.").

    The child, completely incapable of grasping any of this consciously, nevertheless learns to believe: "There must be something wrong with me. That's why they are treating me this way. It's my fault. It's not their fault."

In the child's mind there can't be anything wrong with the adults because survival depends on them.

THIS IS THE BIRTH OF SELF-HATE

5.

The child decides to be "perfect," to do everything right, to be really good in order to be loved. There is no choice about this; the child's survival depends on it.

"They don't love me because there is something wrong with me. I have to think of everything. If I just do it right and never let that happen again, then they'll love me."

THIS SELF-TALK MAINTAINS SELF HATE.

6.

In order to ensure survival, "The Judge" as a subpersonality is born to make sure that the child is perfect and right and good.

The birth of The Judge guarantees the continued existence of self-hate.

This process is constantly repeating up through about age 7 when, it is said, we are completely socialized. After that, The Judge is tenured and guaranteed a full-time job.

During this process we have concluded that needs are bad, and that we are bad for having them.
And, of course, we have them anyway.

Why Am I So Needy?

STUDENT: Recently you used the term "horrible, needy thing," and I realized that that's exactly how I think of it: needy is horrible. No wonder I can't let neediness come up in myself. And when I see it in others, I slam them down with the same judgment that it's horrible and unacceptable.

HORRIBLE
NEEDY
THING
↓

CHERI: That's an example of the conclusion we drew when we first began learning to abandon ourselves. We concluded that the reason we were being rejected was that we had a need, a legitimate, can't-be-helped-that's-just-how-humans-are kind of need. Like being hungry or having to go to the bathroom on a car trip, and getting information that needing something makes you a pain in the butt, and that having a need means you're bad. If you're bad, you're unlovable, and if you're unlovable, you won't be able to survive. So from that perspective, the bottom line is: Don't have needs. Just suck it up, don't say anything, pretend you're okay, be miserable, but don't let anyone know you need anything.

Hint: That's what most adults are doing, which explains why so many adults are cranky and impatient. Their needs are not getting met.

"Nothing worked about the way my folks raised me. When I have kids I'm not going hit them or spit on them. I'm not even going to ground them. I'm going to find a way to help them make good choices without punishing them."

— e

"I don't know why I keep letting my ex-boyfriend lead me into believing he wants me back. I know he's just using me. I don't know why I let my friends go. I'm a lonely nothing with no one who really cares for me. What do I have to do to regain some kind of sanity? I need to be loved. Somebody love me back for once! Help somebody!"

Once we turn our attention outward, away from our own heart and toward someone "out there" who we hope we can please enough that they will meet our needs, most of us never address the original unmet need we were traumatized into abandoning.

Most of us don't know it is that original, unmet need that has been controlling our lives.

The need?

To be loved and accepted exactly as we are.

Conversation with Teens, continued

CH: So, what do you want to tell adults? What should adults know?

--LISTEN. Basically that's it. It would be really nice if people listened to you when you have something to say.

--We need support, some praise, some acknowledgment of the good stuff we do

--Be open to the stuff that's important to us even if its not important to them--not necessarily condone it, but don't say don't do it. Like wanting to be with our friends all the time. My parents may think it's a waste of time, but it's what I want to do and it beats sitting around the house on my butt. So, ok, you think it's a waste of time, but it's what I want to do, so don't give me a hard time about it.

--Don't worry so much about who we hang out with. They just assume that if you're with certain people you're going to be just like those people. They think we have no will power, if someone suggests something or offers us

something, we're going to go along with it automatically. They don't see us as individuals, they see us as who we're with.
--We have good morals, we can make good choices.
--We don't mean any harm. We just want to have fun. We're trying to learn new things.
--Trust us. Talk to us. Get to know us. And trust us.
--You want us to act like adults, treat us with the same respect you give to adults.
--If you want us to respect you, respect us.

CH: In other words, if the teaching is going to be successful, parents have to model what they want you to be.
--Teachers too. The best teachers I've had are the ones who treated us as actual people. I listened to them and excelled in their classes. But the teachers who hate us, the ones who are there for the summers off, I was exactly the opposite. We will be what adults expect us to be.

--You can't just tell us no. Give us a reason. We don't see what you see. We don't understand. You need to explain things to us.

--Don't say, "Because I'm the parent." If you don't have a good reason, if you can't explain it to me, I'm not going to do what you want.

--Adults want to know why. We have to give reasons. Give us the respect you want from us and explain to us your reasons. Tell us why we should do what you want us to do.

--"Because I said so," is not good enough. It makes me <u>have</u> to do the opposite!

--Adults have had a lot of experience we haven't had. Give us the benefit of that experience by explaining what they're thinking, how they see things.

--Give us all the information we need and support us in making a decision.

--Get to know who we are as individuals and support us

--Don't constantly refer to the past and hold the past against us.

--We're not all alike. We're similar, but we are individuals
--Support but don't push
--We're not always going to be children
--We have a lot of emotions inside. Sometimes we don't know what's best for us
--We're not as bad as you think. You were our age once. Give us a break.
--Respect and support our relationships instead of just being freaked out about whether we're having sex
--We're people, too
--Going to your room and closing the door is normal!
--It doesn't matter what you see or hear on the outside, it's what's inside that counts.
-- All teenagers want to have fun. Don't hold us back. Don't live your life through ours.
-- We need privacy and we need attention

To be continued...

Eventually it dawns on us that we can't stay in the "I'm wrong/I'm bad" mode forever or we really won't survive. There has to be a duality formed in which "I'm not wrong; they are wrong" operates.

The sadness is that you can live your whole life trying to prove your parents wrong, but nothing will really have changed. All your ideas about being perfect and right and good will just be in reaction to the conditioning you received from your parents. Not only will you pursue their ideas of perfection, but you will have to reject those ideas, and you will have to reject them perfectly, and pretty soon you will have tied yourself up in such a knot that you won't be able to move in any direction, and you will just sit there in self-hate because the bottom line is

"you lose."

Is there another choice? Yes, you can start seeing that the conclusions you came to about yourself as you were being conditioned to fit into society are not true, real, or accurate. You can start treating yourself the way you wish others would treat you.

"When there's a problem you can't do anything about, that you can't change, parents need to be supportive of their child instead of continuing to have discussion after discussion or fight after fight. Fighting isn't doing anything but making things worse. The negative feelings just continue to increase and you're in a worse situation than before."

Self-Hate Accounting:
The "Insufficient Funds" Rule

STUDENT: Why do I never feel that I have been good enough or generous enough? I try and try but this little nagging guilty feeling is always here.

CHERI: Good question. I look at this a lot. It's just so pervasive in human experience. I was talking about it earlier and gave this example: You go along in life and you do what you're supposed to do. And every time you do something you're supposed to do, you put a dollar in the bank. Okay. Every time you're kind, patient, or you do the thing you're supposed to do--whatever it is (you know what those things are for you) every time, you put a dollar in the bank, a dollar in the bank, a dollar in the bank ...

And you're working at this! You're up early in the morning doing these things until late at night. Every day.

Finally, you feel like you're just kind of worn out. You feel like you need a little pleasure in your life, a little time on the beach or something. And so you think, I'm going to go to the bank, and I'm going to take out some money, and I'm going to do something nice for myself.

So you go to the bank and you say, "Here I am. I want to take out some of the money I've saved so that I can do something nice for myself."

And the response is, "Oh no. You haven't earned nearly enough to get anything for yourself. Oh, you have to work much harder, you have to put much, much more money in before you can get anything for yourself."

REQUEST DENIED
REASON:
INSUFFICIENT FUNDS

Of course, if this were First National you were dealing with, you would say, "No, this is not the way this is going to work. This is my money. You can't tell me when and where and how I can spend it." And yet, at the Bank of Self-Hate, that's exactly what you are told!

With self-hate you get to earn and earn and earn endlessly, and there is never a payback. You think that you're saving up all these points, and that some day you'll receive some benefit from them, but you never do.

STUDENT: Yes. I do that to myself a lot.

CHERI: Let me give you another example. You decide that you're going to take up running. And so this person is going to help you become a runner. You put on your little outfit and the person says, "Why'd you put that on? Boy, do you look stupid in that! You're going to wear that?" Well, you go put on another outfit. You put on several outfits and finally just give up on that discussion. You're never going to <u>look</u> good enough to run so you just decide you're going to do it anyway.

You go out there and start running, and the person says, "You call that running? Whatever made you think you could be a runner?"

Now, I just want to give you another possibility, okay? How about if the person who is with you says, "Run in anything, it doesn't matter. You look fine. Just get out there and run. That's great! You're doing good. How long did you run? Ten minutes? That's wonderful!"

Think about it! Which person wants you to run, and which person wants you not to run?

There's no mystery in this, folks!

It's not hard to pick out which characters are in which camp. Internally or externally! In the first example, the person at the Bank of Self-Hate DOES NOT LIKE YOU!

It's important to get that!

It's not like this person is really pulling for you to get enough money in the bank to do something special for yourself.
NO!
This person is never going to give you a dime!
You will work yourself to death, and you'll never get a thing for it.

It is really important to understand that!

If you had a person
in your life

treating you the way
        you treat yourself,

        you would have gotten
        rid of them

            a long
                time
                    ago...

STUDENT: You'd think so, wouldn't you?

CHERI: It seems so clear, but because that voice speaks from inside our own heads, we are actually willing to perpetuate the illusion that this person who calls us names, who says mean and hateful things to us:
- is on our side
- likes us
- has something valuable to say
- has some sort of merit in life.

But it isn't and it doesn't!

You do not want to let someone who does not like you run your life.

You don't let it pick your friends.

You don't let it make decisions about your school work.

You don't let it decide what you're going to do.

You don't let it interact with parents and teachers.

It doesn't like you and it will talk you into doing things that will make you really miserable and then try to convince you that doing those things was your idea! Are you with me?

STUDENT: I am with you. Sometimes I don't see that separation. Right now, right here in this room, it seems very clear to me.

CHERI: I can give you the simplest of all possible rules of thumb: Any time a voice is talking to you without love and compassion, don't believe it!
   Even if it is talking about someone else, don't believe it. Even if it is directed at someone else, it is the voice of your self-hate. It is simply hating you through an external object. It can hate you directly by telling you what a lousy, rotten person you are, and it can hate you indirectly by pointing out what's wrong with someone else. Either way, you feel bad.

If the voice is not loving, don't listen to it, don't follow it, don't believe it.
   No exceptions!

Even if it says it's "for your own good," it is not. It's for its good, not yours. This is the same as when parents talk to you in a hateful tone of voice "for your own good." It's for their good. It makes them feel better. It does not make you better. And it does not make you behave "better." I bet you've noticed that! Parents talk to you in a hateful way and all you want to do is the opposite of whatever they say.

Conversation with Teens, continued

CH: Again, it comes down to intelligent conversation.

B: Yeah, instead of, "Don't have sex. It's bad to have sex." Except for my dad who says, "Go out there and get all you can get."

L: That would scare me. I couldn't deal if my folks said that to me.

CH: So, where does that leave you with AIDS?

B: My dad probably has AIDS. If he doesn't, it's not because he hasn't tried. He's weak.

CH: Is it hard for you to respect someone like your dad?

B: I have no respect for him at all.

V: I wish they would stop judging us on the past actions of others.

CH: Like themselves?

V: Yeah, but even more, like the whole Columbine thing. I just read about a kid who got suspended, then expelled, for drawing a gun in the corner of his paper. Just a gun. Not someone being shot, not someone wielding a gun, a technical drawing of a gun.

G: Years ago I took to school some of those things you put in the end of cigarettes that when you light them make the cigarette explode, and they expelled me.

CH: And no one talked to you about it?

G: Nope, they just sent me home.

CH: So, you're expected to anticipate the fears adults have?

T: Yeah, and their fears are insane. My little sister got sent home from school for wearing red shoe laces. Red is a gang color and you can't wear red to school. My little sister! They're idiots! You can't wear red or blue. What if a gang starts wearing orange or yellow or green and we can't wear those colors. Pretty soon we won't be able to wear any colors. We'll have to go to school naked.

Group: Okay! Yeah! Fine with me! I see no problem with that!

B: I have a friend who's half African-American and half white. My family took me aside and asked, "Is he in a gang?" Even though he doesn't dress like it or look like it or talk like it. They're stupid.

CH: Well, why does something like Columbine happen?

R: Because nobody listens. Because there's a lack of respect. Because only people who fit into a certain narrow definition of "right" are treated with respect. If you're not a jock, if you're not one of the "smart" people, if you're not "popular," people treat you like you're a lesser life form. Eventually lesser life forms strike back.

T: But the people who are going to pull a gun are not the ones drawing guns on the corner of their paper. They're going to hide out, and you're never going to know they're thinking anything until they do it.

G: That's what scares the crap out of adults; they can't control it at all. And everything they do to try to control it just makes them look like the idiots they are.

X: I wore a black trench coat for years and people harried me so much I thought, "Are they trying to make me kill them?" They're such fools!

To be continued

Here are some outrageous things I suggest about this. Any time you hear the voice of self-hate, do something for yourself that will make it crazy. If the voice says you're ugly or fat or stupid or a loser, go out and buy yourself a present. Sit down and read for pleasure. Call a friend who is kind to you. Go to a movie.

STUDENT: Whatever it is that you can't let yourself do.

CHERI: Yes. Whatever would be lazy and indulgent...

STUDENT: ...thoughtless, selfish...

CHERI: <u>YES!</u> The more, the better. It can be as simple as going for a walk on a nice day. You just keep walking until the voice is still, until it is clear that it's not in control anymore. Then, when you're ready, when you're present, when you are once again who you <u>really</u> are, not who self-hate accuses you of being, go back to your regular life.

Constructive Criticism: Not Required

Let's say that you sense you have been less than kind toward someone. The voice of constructive criticism says quietly, "That was pretty harsh. You're too sarcastic. You always have been. You better clean up your act before you alienate everyone."

This voice justifies itself by saying things like, "I'm just trying to point these things out to you so that you'll be a better, kinder, happier person."

BUT

"constructive criticism" is a scam run by people (internal and external) who want to beat you up. And they want you to believe that they're doing it for your own good! They would have you believe that without their "constructive criticism," you would always be harsh and sarcastic.

Be suspicious of any voice
inside or outside
that says,
"There is something wrong with you."

This voice does not like you and is not helpful.

It is possible that with the awareness that you have been unkind toward someone, you might realize, in a gentle sort of way, "I don't want to do that. It doesn't feel very good." So it's not that you're a bad person, or even that you shouldn't have said what you said; it's just that you don't want to be unkind because it hurts your heart.

When you are open to that awareness, you won't need to try to be different, for in that gentle approach,
                you will already have changed.

COMMON WISDOM
that supports self-hate

It is more blessed to give than to receive.

You can't teach an old dog new tricks.

The lyrics to "Santa Claus Is Coming To Town."

You get what you deserve.

The harder you try, the better you'll do.

Two heads are better than one.

Some things are just meant to be.

If you are not the lead dog, the view never changes.

Children should be seen and not heard.

Do as I say, not as I do.

ADD YOUR OWN:

CONFLICTING BELIEFS
that maintain self-hate

Patience is a virtue.
Strike while the iron is hot.

I am my brother's keeper.
Look out for Number One.

Neither a borrower nor a lender be.
Generosity is a virtue.

Carpe diem. (Seize the day.)
Save for a rainy day.

Be realistic.
Be imaginative.

Express yourself.
Control yourself.

ADD YOUR OWN:

Conversation with Teens, continued

CH: Any adult say anything meaningful?

"You can be different."

"I trust you."

My English teacher said he realized how much he hated the ignorance of other people and vowed that he would learn not to be one of those ignorant people rather than just hating them.

"You have all the answers inside yourself."

"Don't cry because it ended, smile because it happened."

A teacher said, "Do it right the first time and get on with it. Don't fool around, screw up, and then have to go back and fix it." I figure that applies to all life, not just math.

"Don't waste your time wishing, go out and make those wishes come true."

"You can change what others do only by changing what you do."

"Follow your heart"

"Everything you feel and say is important."

"You only live once."

"Children learn what they live."

" We learn from every mistake we make in life so don't be afraid to make them."

To be continued...

Self-Evaluation: Another Unhelpful Idea

Self-hate is

LIFE'S LITTLE REPORT CARD

DOING IT RIGHT	A+
BEING ATTENTIVE	A+
MAKING DECISIONS	A+
HELPING OTHERS	A+
BEING SUCCESSFUL	A+
HANDLING PRESSURE	D-

putting incredible pressure on myself
to be perfect
which causes me to make mistakes* because I'm
so stressed and overwhelmed and miserable.

*Remember: It isn't actually possible to make mistakes.
Mistake is what self-hate calls learning.

Conversation with Teens, continued

CH: What about mistakes?
--If you don't make mistakes how are you supposed to learn?
--Now is the best time to make mistakes. You're not old enough to go to prison!
--The other day I had to go register for junior college. I've never had to register for anything before, my mom has always done it. She said, "you do it, you're eighteen." Then the next day I broke a glass and she yelled at me like I was a little kid. So I don't get to screw up like a little kid, and I don't have the information I need to be an adult.
--We're going to make mistakes, give us a chance to clean them up.
--These are not mistakes, we're learning!

To be continued...

Investing in Misery

STUDENT: I'm aware that I tend to focus on punishment and not notice reward. I seem to believe that punishment works and reward doesn't. I wonder what I get from having this belief.

CHERI: If you believe that punishment works then it makes sense to do a bunch of stuff you consider wrong so you can be punished a lot and life will "work" according to your beliefs.

STUDENT: It seems I have an investment in misery.

CHERI: Keep in mind that egocentricity, self-hate, and misery are synonymous. To be miserable is to be the center of the universe. Now let's add the ingredient of feeling oneself to be innocent and yet punished. "I may have done something wrong, but it wasn't THAT bad. Surely I don't deserve THIS!"

Ok, so I failed that class.
  So I got a speeding ticket.
    So, I wrecked the car.
I don't deserve all this punishment! It's not my fault!!!

Isn't that perfect? We even use our misdeeds to our advantage. I've done something I know I shouldn't have, but I've turned it around so that I am the victim and should be compensated. And self-hate is usually right there with suggestions that could make up for this injustice. Things like:

- ice cream
- not returning a wallet you find
- driving discourteously
- gossiping
- having an affair with someone else's partner

 "After all, life owes me something for this injustice." "After all, I've been treated unfairly and I'm owed big."

Self-Hate Accounting System

In the self-hate accounting system:
- I add up everything I do. I subtract everything everyone else doesn't do.
- I add up everything everyone else gets. I subtract everything that I don't get.
- I add up all the luck everybody else has. I subtract all the luck I don't have.
- I add up all the advantages everybody else had. I subtract all the advantages I didn't have.

You get the picture.

I am so far in the hole because all I do is good things and all I get is bad things.

So how can I not feel myself to be a victim? And why should I not try to even the score?

And, of course, what we fail to see is that almost everyone sees themselves as victims and others as victimizers so people continue to victimize one another.

Who of us will stop?

> "But wait a minute. It seems to me that the people who are supposed to love me, do want me to feel inadequate, unworthy, and undeserving. They're only interested in what I'm doing wrong. Then when I do something right, they just bring up something else wrong I did. But they're never willing to admit they do anything wrong. They just want to degrade you for everything bad, never praise you for anything good."

As a teenager, parents and teachers (all adults, in fact) are telling me what to do, pushing me around all the time. If I just look at all the ways they're unfair to me and don't notice all the good things they're doing for me, I can feel like everyone is picking on me, I'm not doing anything wrong, they're getting all the good stuff, I'm getting all the bull, and I deserve to retaliate, to get back at them, through any means at my disposal. They deserve it! Of course, it makes me miserable to live that way, but when I'm looking at the world from that "I'm good/they're bad" place, I can't stop myself from trying to get back at them. Hint: As soon as I get it that I'm the one suffering in my attempts to get back at them, I no longer want to do that to myself.

Self-Hate and The Battering Cycle

In relationships, the stresses of life can lead one person to become physically or verbally abusive toward the other. This can result in a cyclical pattern of behavior that includes the following elements: increasing stress, abuse, contrition, and a decision to "be perfect."

We often think of the battering cycle happening between a man and a woman, but it can happen with any two or more people. We often see it in families. In the form of self-hate, it requires only oneself.

In the classic situation, a man and a woman get married because they want to make their lives better. He will take care of her, and she will be supportive of him.

After a while, it stops working. The stresses of life push him to a crisis point, and he relieves his frustration by beating her. Then he feels good because his stress is relieved, but he feels bad because he beat his wife.

She feels good because she has been punished for letting him down, but she feels bad because her husband just beat her.

Then they get together and decide that this awful thing must never happen again, and they both feel better.

They have a plan. It's under control. "We won't make that mistake again. We'll do better. We'll be perfect."

And the stress begins to build again...

It is easy to see how this pattern gets established at an early age for children in their families. Children are little "meet-my-needs machines." It's biological, programmed in to make sure children survive. It is true in all species. The young are focused on whatever they need to guarantee their survival. Children are not aware of, nor can they comprehend, how stressful it is to be an adult trying to make it in the world: earn money, keep a job, maintain a household, buy and cook food, do laundry, pay bills, keep up relationship responsibilities, be a good citizen, etc. It is a huge, mostly unrewarding job. The child doesn't know any of this or care about it. The child's "job" is to get whatever is needed in each moment to survive: attention, food, protection. The parent sees their own overwhelming responsibility, views the child as the recipient of all the hard work the parent is doing, says to the child, "Can't you at least clean up your room? Can't you hang up the clothes I'm working myself to death to provide for you?" By the time a child is a teenager, often before, the answer, stated or unstated, is "No!" The parent goes ballistic. Punishment is meted out. The parent feels better because some of that awful stress is released in the blow up. The child feels better because there is a lot of guilt and anxiety that accompanies not pleasing the parent and that badness has now been punished. But both parent and child feel bad because they love one another and they've just acted in a really unloving way toward one another.

So the steps are:
  Stresses build
  There's a conflict
  Explosion
  Relief
  Feel better/feel worse
  Stress starts building
  Repeat

Addictive behaviors, whether it's food, alcohol, drugs, sex, smoking, achieving, or relationships follow the same cycle.

FOR EXAMPLE:

The stresses of life begin to build, and I reach for my addiction of choice. If it's food, I head for the kitchen and eat my way from one end to the other. I feel good because the stress is relieved. I have kind of anesthetized myself, and the craving is calmed. But I feel AWFUL because I have just eaten a ton!

So I beat myself until I'm convinced that I've got a grip on it. I see what happened. It will never happen again. I have a program. I've got it right this time. I'm going to do better. In fact, I'll be perfect.

And the stress begins to build...

THE BATTERING CYCLE

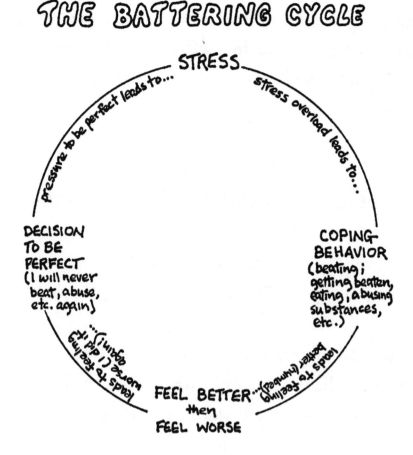

STRESS

pressure to be perfect leads to...

stress overload leads to...

DECISION
TO BE
PERFECT
(I will never
beat, abuse,
etc. again)

COPING
BEHAVIOR
(beating;
getting beaten,
eating, abusing
substances,
etc.)

leads to feeling worse (I did it again!)...

leads to feeling better (numbed)...

FEEL BETTER...
then
FEEL WORSE

This process can happen
- between two people
- within ourselves (between two parts
  or subpersonalities)

Adopting the belief that you must be perfect is the perfect set up for self-hate. You believe that your choices are to be perfect or to be a failure.

BUT SELF-HATE
SETS THE STANDARD OF PERFECTION

and you can bet
you are never going to meet that standard.

If you did, if you met that standard, what would self-hate beat you with? What would it frighten you with? And if you weren't frightened, how would you be controlled?

Self-hate would have you
believe that either it is in
control, making you be who and
how you should be, or not only
will you be imperfect, you will
be garbage.

It has convinced you that if you were to be just how you are, you would be awful.

So the

BIG, UGLY LIE
BECOMES BIG, UGLY BELIEF:

Self-hate, judgment, blame, punishment, and rejection are all for your benefit because they're the only things keeping you from being

A TERRIBLE PERSON.
(Have we made our point?)

Would you please risk it and find out once and for all how you are WITHOUT the beatings and abuse?

Unconditional Love

STUDENT: Yesterday I was thinking that if I'm going to learn to love myself, I need to learn to love myself just the way I am. It occurred to me that even being overweight, I need to be thankful for this opportunity to love myself. It comforts me to think I might be this way for a reason and that reason might be to learn to love myself.

CHERI: Yes. Even if you lost weight and had a "perfect body," but had not learned to love yourself, where would you be?

STUDENT: I would still be trying to improve myself, to fix the things that I think are wrong.

CHERI: You will still be believing that as long as you do it right, look a certain way, act the way you should, accomplish certain things, you'll be lovable.

But can you be lovable not meeting the standards?

Can you be a best friend to this person who does not meet the standards that you were taught must be met before you can be lovable?

Can you stop trying to change into who you wish you were long enough to find out who you really are?

You will never improve yourself enough to meet your standards. Self-hate will see to that. But the moment you love yourself, you are completely changed. You will always have a friend. You will never be alone.

Conversation with Teens, continued

CH: Who do you trust?

-- No one.

-- I don't trust my parents.

-- I trust my friends. I enjoy being myself. I think it's important to be an individual. We're similar in that we share issues, but we are still who we are as a person. And we respect one another.

-- I trust my family. They've always been with me.

-- I don't trust anyone. I'm not sure why, I just don't and can't.

To be continued...

> "With friends, we all have the same definition for 'best friend'--trustworthy, caring, honest, friendly. We trust each other with secrets and we're there for each other."

Not wanting to be how you are
is one of the most significant aspects
of self-hate.

If I am disapproving of myself,
I am giving myself information that
who I am is not okay.

That's self-hate.

Enjoy It All

We have been conditioned to believe that it's not okay to feel what we feel or think what we think or have the experiences we're having. As children, people didn't like us as we were so they tried to change us. We've internalized that process, and we've taken on that system of "self-improvement" ourselves. So now we're trying to change everything we don't approve of.

In acceptance, we don't want to change anything about ourselves. It's only in non-acceptance that we hope acceptance will mean that the way we are will change.

"Okay, I'll accept the fact that I don't always think before I speak, and then maybe I won't be that way anymore." That kind of "acceptance" is non-acceptance and it won't work.

With acceptance we can have
the full range of experience
that is our potential,
and we can enjoy it all.

We will finally be free to be all the ways we are, even the ways other people didn't like and tried to get rid of.

If we move through and beyond the belief that we need to change, then everything is available to us. If you're miserable, there's nothing really wrong with that, but if you're hating being miserable, then it's hell. If you're miserable and not hating it, 1) you're not miserable, you're accepting, and 2) you'll probably move through it pretty quickly.

Experiences do move along quickly when we're present. It's when we stop being present and get stuck in something that we can drag it out forever.

We are never going to "get" something,

a philosophy,
a formula,
a fixed point of view
that will make us forever different.

There is no secret that will fix you.

(Remember,
there is nothing wrong with you.)

This is a lifelong process. If you decide to learn to care for yourself, to live your life in compassion, you will be required to practice that until you die.

An internal relationship must be worked on and maintained just like an external relationship.

And that's good news!

When you fall in love with someone, you don't say, "Oh, no, how long am I going to have to love this person?"

When we're in love, we love to love that person, and we hope it will last forever.

Advantages of Ending Self-Hate

When you don't hate yourself, you won't
be chronically late,
be chronically early,
procrastinate,
study compulsively,
abuse substances,
deprive yourself,
depress your feelings,
try to be perfect,
worry too much,
worry about worrying too much,
depend on other's approval,
believe your Judge,
reject your Judge,
punish yourself,
overindulge yourself,
pass up opportunities,
be afraid of yourself,
try to improve,
try to improve others,
Add your own:

We are responsible for being
the person we've always wanted to find.

We must become our own best friend.

We must learn to give to ourselves
and
to receive from ourselves
unconditional love and acceptance.

It is not selfish.
It is the first
GIANT STEP
toward selfLESSness.

We call people selfish

>   when they WILL not give.
>   But they CANNOT give
>   what they DO NOT have.

It's like asking a starving child to share her food,
and then making her feel guilty
for not wanting to.

When we have enough we are eager to share.

> "Give kids a chance. The more rules you set the
> more we want to break. The better morals you
> give us and raise us with the more we will stay true
> to those. Keep connected. Talking isn't easy but it
> gets you through some hard (silent) issues and
> makes life better."

THOSE WHO FEEL
COMPLETELY LOVED
ARE NOT SELFISH,
THEY ARE LOVING.

Nothing to Do

What we're seeing here is how the layers of self-hate keep us from experiencing our intrinsic, inherent perfection. It's simply a matter of realizing what already is. It's not necessary for us to DO anything. What we're seeking is available to us when we stop DOING everything else.

> We don't have to change.
> We don't have to fix ourselves.
> We don't have to improve.
> We don't have to do it right.

What we are seeking is who we already are.

> "Be what you're asking us to be. Be responsible. Be honest. Be polite. Be respectful. Adults have one set of standards for us and another one for themselves."

We don't need to DO anything.

To let ourselves be
in compassionate acceptance
is all that is required.

There is a small child inside each of us who was taught to believe that bad things happen, or will happen, because s/he is bad.

As we are older, if we become aware of this child, we are saddened and we feel the child's sadness. We are conditioned to try to STOP the sadness, to move away from the experience.

The child doesn't need for us to do that. The child needs to know, deep down inside, that it is absolutely all right to be having that experience. The child needs complete acceptance for however s/he is in each moment. And as we grow up, we do, too. That's what we didn't get when we were little--acceptance for however we are in whatever moment.

What works is compassion. Trying to STOP,

FIX or CHANGE is part of the self-hating process.

Just stay with the experience and
REALLY GET IT
that this is <u>sad,</u>
it's not wrong,
it's just sad,
it's hard to be a human.
How can we not feel compassion?

Of course, self-hate will jump right in there and say, "Enough of this sadness. Let's DO something about it."

But trying to do something will flip us right back into the bottom of the pot. I imagine a big stew pot of self-hate, and you just about crawl up to the  top of the pot when you run into something that flips you right back in.

Usually this "something" is trying to change what you are experiencing. Criticizing yourself, judging somebody else, thinking you need to change something, fix something, DO something, and you are right back in the bottom of the pot of self-hate again.

Trying to do something about a situation keeps us stuck in that situation. Accepting where we are allows us to move along in life. How does that work? Resistance is what keeps us stuck. When we don't resist, life flows along from thing to thing to thing. It's like surfing. If you relax and go with the movement, it's easy. If you get scared, tense up, want something to be different from the way it is, SPLASH, you go under.

> 'I was happy when I was little. My parents were nice to me and they played with me.'

Gratitude

If you find it difficult to catch the subtler self-hating processes at work, it can be helpful to take some time to be alone and quiet, perhaps to sit in meditation. One of the ways we can see self-hate in an awareness practice goes something like this:

You're sitting there,
just breathing,
paying attention,
quiet,
still.

You begin to notice that even though all you are doing is sitting silently and breathing, a part of you is constantly scanning, trying to find just the thing that will

pull you away

from the stillness.

It says things like:

This continues until something hooks you and your attention wanders. Soon you realize that you have been daydreaming/fantasizing/worrying/problem solving and you bring your attention back to the breath.

Now this is another perfect place to see self-hate at work.

Self-hate will try to get you to believe that you've done something wrong because your attention wandered. Don't fall for it!

Your attention wanders. You realize it and come back to the breath. Don't waste your time and energy beating yourself up for having wandered. Just sit quietly in gratitude for having returned.

Self-Hate's Greatest Talent

Self-hate's greatest talent is self-maintenance. It carries on a thorough, aggressive, sometimes loud, sometimes quiet, often subtle campaign to keep us in its grip.

It would justify itself by claiming that it enables us to survive. That is a delusion.

We do not need to beat, punish, discipline, chastise, berate, and belittle ourselves and we never did. THE IRONIC TWIST IS THAT PUNISHING OURSELVES IS WHAT KEEPS US FROM SEEING THAT WE DON'T NEED TO PUNISH OURSELVES. If we can ever become aware and willing enough to break the internal battering cycle and NOT INDULGE IN THE BEATING, we can begin to see how this is so. It takes courage and patience and faith in our inherent goodness.

PAINFUL THINGS COME UP
NOT TO RUIN OUR LIVES,
NOT TO MAKE US MISERABLE,
NOT TO SPOIL OUR GOOD TIME,

THEY COME UP IN ORDER TO BE HEALED,
TO BE EMBRACED IN COMPASSION.

We often wish our childhood survival system
would just go away, but once we have embraced
it, once we've realized how much it has done for
us and how much we've learned because of it,
we are grateful it kept up the clamor.

"If I could change one thing about
the way I was raised it would be to
get more education about sex and
drugs at an earlier age, like 5th or
6th grade."

Self-hate is

getting a new car
and not taking care of it.*

*"Not taking care of" is not taking care of <u>yourself</u>.

Self-hate is

eating the dessert I want

and calling myself names like
"fat pig" or "slob."

STUDENT: Coming here today a voice was saying, "Nobody wants to hear what you have to say." Of course no one, including me, knew what I was going to say, but that doesn't stop that voice. Now that I'm here and I haven't said anything, the voice is saying, "You're not participating. You should be talking."

CHERI: So, whatever you're doing is wrong; whatever you did was wrong; and whatever you're going to do will be wrong.

Using a system like that to stay safe is a case of the cure being worse than the disease.

Self-hate is

torturing myself with "It's not fair."

I see what my friends get to do and have and how their parents are, then I look at how hard I try and how little effort my parents make, and I say, "It's unfair."

But my situation is what it is, and if I weren't torturing myself with unfairness, I wouldn't be suffering. Instead I stay stuck in this feeling that I'm being mistreated.

To compound the self-hating mess, I'm paralyzed because I'm afraid to bring any of this up, and I hate myself for being afraid.

Self-Hate and Addiction

Self-hate coping behaviors
make you feel better
and
make you feel worse
at the same time.

All major addictions are like this.

Self-hate is the ultimate addiction.

If you think self-hate isn't an addiction,

try to stop.

CHERI: Self-hate is an addiction and a lot of self-hate is accomplished through other addictions.

I was talking to someone last night who had been sober for four and a half years and had gone out and had a drink. I told her that when she no longer hates herself, she won't need to do that. When you don't hate yourself, you don't want to mistreat yourself. It's as simple as that.

With an addiction like alcohol, there has to come a time when you sit at the kitchen table with a bottle in front of you, and you sit there until you know you're not going to drink. Like the movie <u>High Noon</u>, you've got to go out and face the Bad Guy. You may get lucky, or you may not, but you have to go out there for the showdown or pretty soon the bad guys are going to run the town. You can't hope that self-hate is going to get tired of beating you up and go away. Like blackmail, once the extortion starts, it's going to bleed you for everything you've got and then it's going to leave you for dead. It's not going to take your last dime and then leave; this isn't just turning off the faucet, it's ripping the plumbing out.

So do you want to take a chance with a confrontation, or do you want to just die a slow, lingering death? With the first choice you have a 50/50 chance; with the second, you have none. To stay with this analogy/parable/eulogy...you actually have a much better than 50/50 chance, because as soon as you strap on your six-shooter and start walking down Main Street at high noon, the Bad Guy isn't going to show up.

STUDENT: Right. Nothing bears up under scrutiny. In fact, nothing shows up under scrutiny.

CHERI: But if you're quaking in hiding, you'll never make it to Main Street. As FDR said, "We have nothing to fear but fear itself." We are so afraid of being afraid, we are so afraid that we will be inadequate, that we won't prove to ourselves that we're not. The one who is projecting the inadequacy--in one of our previous scenes--says things like, "You think you're going to be a runner?" It's a different situation so it's sometimes hard to see that it's coming from the same source.

But who is invested in your being afraid? In maintaining an illusion of inadequacy? Do people who love you want you to be afraid? Want you to experience yourself as inadequate, unworthy, and undeserving? No, not at all.

Once we realize that fear is a process, we can get a handle on it. And there's nothing that's going to push you into this any faster than confronting the self-hate in the way that I've described, because terror will arise. Every time a hateful voice comes up and starts telling you something, you just sit on the couch and read a book, or go out and look at flowers, or call your best friend, or go to a movie.

STUDENT: Then terror arises?

CHERI: YES. SELF-HATE IS TERRIFIED THAT YOU WILL MAKE BEING KIND TO YOURSELF A HABIT.

It comes down to this for me: None of my heroes (and all my heroes are spiritual types) ever says, "The important thing in the universe is to be at one with fear and inadequacy." Okay? Nobody has ever defined God as "fear and inadequacy," and then said that is what you should strive for. And so, if I'm going to hold Awareness, True Nature, Buddha Nature, God as the greatest value in life and then on a moment by moment basis choose the opposite of that, then what am I doing? This is the fundamental issue. How can I go beyond this fear in order to choose the wisdom, love and compassion that I know is possible for me?

STUDENT: Yes, how does one get beyond that?

CHERI: For me, I go back to "putting the bottle on the table." I have times in my life of sitting on my meditation cushion and holding onto it because that's the only way I can avoid screaming or suicide or madness as every bit of my conditioning comes up inside of me and says the hateful stuff it says.

St. John of the Cross talked about the dark night of the soul, and to me this was exactly what he is talking about. His image of it was God and the devil wrestling for your immortal soul. And isn't that what it feels like? And doesn't it seem, most of the time, like the devil is winning?

STUDENT: Yeah. It could even look like I'm on the devil's side!

CHERI: Yes, and so for me, and this is where I depart from a lot of the rest of

the world, I really don't believe for a minute that there is something more important than that which I am seeking. I don't think there is anything more important! I don't think money is more important, I don't think security is more important, or a good reputation, or being popular, or having people like me, or anything else. I don't think there is anything more important than my True Nature, than learning to live from who I truly am. So if something is coming between me and that, I am going to pay attention until it is no longer there. I am simply going to stay conscious, and keep coming back to what I know is true, until there is nothing between me and that truth. I know when that is. We all know when that is. We all know that moment of oneness with our True Nature, the peace, the joy, the comfort. We know when we're there, and we know when we're not. (You may be hearing a voice that says. "I don't. I don't know when that is." And that's perfect, that's the voice that's trying to stand between you and the experience of your True Nature.)

It's like discord in a relationship with someone I love. I am going to turn my attention to the discord until that lack of harmony is gone and peace, joy and comfort are back. I don't say, "I'll look at that later." I want to look at it NOW! I don't want to look at anything else until that's resolved, and I know the resolution of it is in here (points to heart). So I'm required to pay attention to it.

With my kids I want to teach them about life before their friends start teaching them. If they need to be punished I want to punish them in a way that doesn't make them feel bad about themselves. I'm going to listen to them more and do more things with them.

Self-hate is like quicksand.

Everything you do to try to get out
causes you to sink deeper.

Every place you step
to try to avoid the place you're in,
also pulls you down.

In quicksand, if you cease struggling, you will sink
more slowly.

In self-hate, when you cease to struggle
(when you accept),
you are free.

Compassion, No Matter What

STUDENT: This is a pattern of self-hate I've noticed. Lately, I've been trying to say, "Okay, I have this need and I'm going to stand up for myself this time. I'm going to ask for what I want." So I do it, and my worst fears come true. People don't like what I said or did. My need is rejected. Then self-hate comes in and says, "I warned you!" But then another voice that it hasn't been possible for me to hear before says, "But you did it. That's the important thing this time. It doesn't matter what happened afterwards, you did it."

CHERI: Yes, we see the self-hate patterns and we practice with them. We learn not to believe those voices. They aren't going to stop, they're going to continue. And they're going to hit a level heretofore unimagined, because when you start trying to break this stuff up, it will escalate. When you start picking away at the foundation of self-hate, it's going to bring out everything in the world to defend itself. We can count on that. It's when things are hardest for us and compassion is most needed that self-hate is strongest.

Because if you can have compassion for yourself in a time when you really need it, if you can be a friend to yourself when it feels like nobody is on your side, can you imagine how powerful that would be and how the self-hate system would begin to shake and crumble? You can't have too many of those experiences without beginning to question whether all of this self-hate is actually accomplishing what it's saying it's intended to accomplish. That's why the answer is <u>compassion, no matter what.</u>

Now, what we often say is that we can have compassion as long as it's not a Really Terrible Thing we've done. But that's when we need compassion most!

STUDENT: So if you've really blown it, really done your worst, and all the self-hate voices come up, then the compassion needs to accept even those voices...

CHERI: When we stop seeing them as powerful, when we see them instead as pathetic, as lost and hurting and misguided, how could we not have compassion?

"I wish my parents had told us more about what goes on. I wish they had kept promises. I'm going to trust my kids first."

Willingness Is the Key

STUDENT: Something that has made a difference for me in understanding acceptance is realizing that things don't have to change for me to accept them. If something is happening, all I have to do is be willing to acknowledge that, and that is accepting it. Accepting is not the same as condoning. All acceptance means is "Yes, I can see that this is happening." It's not as if my acceptance or non-acceptance can change whether it happens or not. It's already happening, and all I need do is acknowledge it.

CHERI: I can't make any of this happen but I can show up and be available. To me that's what awareness practice is--the willingness to show up and be available. It's like having your hands open to receive. There's no guarantee that you'll get anything, but if anybody wants to give you something, you're ready.

STUDENT: I am not consistent or disciplined about doing formal meditation, but I am consistently willing to look at my "stuff" and to use the world as a mirror in which I can see my projections. This helps me acknowledge that there are parts of myself that I don't like and that I am afraid of.

CHERI: That's the crux of the whole thing because the basis of awareness practice is ending suffering, and at every moment we have the opportunity to see what in us is suffering. We can ask, "What is outside the realm of compassion? What is not cared for?" And we can bring that into the healing light of compassion by simply acknowledging it, accepting it, allowing it. For instance, I tend to lose my temper; I procrastinate with my homework; I don't like my younger siblings. This is the kind of person I am. This exists in me. I feel this, I do this. I have these thoughts. I have these tendencies. <u>The conditioned patterns of suffering would have us hide this information so</u>

<u>that they continue to exist outside the healing light of compassion.</u> But only to the degree that we can find the willingness to bring them into that light can they be healed.

We must learn to be with ourselves as we would be with our best friend. If your best friend said, "I lose my temper a lot," you wouldn't say, "You are a horrible person, you should feel bad and guilty, and I never want to see you again." You would accept those feelings in your friend. You would know your friend is a good person AND feels those feelings. Same with you.

In that way, you can have all of you, instead of trying to put out only those things that self-hate tells you are acceptable. You can BE, you can EXPERIENCE, you can HAVE everything, just being who you are in the moment.

STUDENT: In spite of knowing how joyful it is to have that happen, it's still terrifying to find another aspect of myself I've never seen.

CHERI: Yes, because self-hate sees that as a threat. As long as there are those awful hidden things in you, self-hate can control your behavior. When you're willing to let everything come into the light of day, self-hate no longer has any power over you.

It's just like blackmail. People can be blackmailed only if they have a secret they want to keep. If I want to hide something I think is awful, and you find out what that thing is, I will pay you anything to keep you from telling. If I just go ahead and tell on myself, you can't hold anything over my head, and I don't have to pay you a dime. I'm free!

If I could have compassion
(love myself)
for hating myself
(!)

I would no longer be hating myself,
I'd be loving myself

and nothing about me would need to
change.

The Voices: Listen, but Don't Believe

It's helpful to develop a habit of not believing any of the voices. That way you can listen to any of them. Listen, but not believe. In the same way, you can sit around the table at lunch with a group of friends who are all talking. You can listen to them, but you don't have to decide who is right and who is wrong. It's not necessary at the lunch table, and it's not necessary within yourself. You can just have the attitude of being present but not involved. The attitude of mind is one of, "Is that so?"

When you can have that attitude of mind with other people, it's a big step. When you can have it within yourself, you're moving toward freedom. Because as all this yakkety-yak goes on in your head, you think you have to figure out which is right and which is wrong. But the part of you who's <u>trying to figure that out is the problem</u>. That's the person who is confused and suffering. When you can step back and listen to the voices in your head instead of believing them, there isn't anything to figure out, and there's nothing to believe. There's just being fully present in the moment.

The voices take us out of the moment and make us believe there is a world other than the present. The more they can get us involved in that belief, the more we're going to believe in the illusion of ourselves as separate, and the more we're going to suffer. The less we believe, the less we are seduced, the more we're able to be in the present, and the less there is someone to suffer.

"When did I feel happiest? Strangely enough when I was sitting in a car, just thinking. I realized everything was amazing. Everything is made up from something else. Everything we use was made by someone to make our lives easier."

Learn to be present.

Practice hearing the voices in your head without becoming involved and without judgment.
And take it on faith that any voice, internal or external, that is telling you that

SOMETHING IS WRONG WITH YOU

is not the voice of your
Heart,
God,
True Nature.

The simple, astounding,
Mind-bogglingly amazing
FACT
is that as soon as you accept yourself
EXACTLY AS YOUR ARE
all your "character flaws"

AGGRESSIVE
SELFISH
SNOBBISH
RECLUSIVE
SHY
ANGRY
DEPENDENT
INSECURE
STRESSFUL

begin to fall away
because those "flaws" have their
only existence in non-acceptance,
in self-hate.

CHERI: Nothing about how you are is a problem until you resist it. The problem comes into existence with resistance.

STUDENT: But what if I want to do something that's harmful?

CHERI: Wanting to do something and doing something are two entirely different things. There's no need to act just because you have a feeling.

STUDENT: But what if I want to act?

CHERI: Your questions come from a belief that you are inherently bad, and that if you don't control yourself, you'll be bad. When you realize that you are goodness and let yourself live from that, being harmful, intentionally harmful, would never occur to you.

If you take the
most frightening
thing in the world

and invite it in,

put your arms
around it,

and sit still
with it,

what is left
to be frightened by?

Self-Hate: Everyone's Doing It!

Once I catch on to how this self-hate process works, I see that it goes on all the time, everywhere.

Everyone does it. This is just how we operate as socially conditioned human beings. When I see this to be true, self-hate ceases to be a private, secret thing I do that proves I'm a bad person. As I realize everyone does it, everyone was conditioned the same way, I can begin to take it less personally.

At some point,
now or later, you're going to have to risk
being you
in order to find out
who that really is.

Not the conditioned you, not the "you" you've been taught to believe you are, but who you really are.

And this perhaps will be the scariest, the most loving, the most rewarding thing you have ever done.

If you are not becoming kinder,
gentler,
more generous,
and loving,
you are not doing this work.

If you are feeling more burdened,
judgmental,
and rejected,
you are doing self-hate.

"I would like to be just like my mom when I grow up.
She always seems to know what to do in every
situation and how to handle every little thing life
throws at her. She can always give me the best
advice when I'm in a fight with one of my friends or
when I just need a boost to my spirits."

What Is the Path?

We find the model on the following pages to be a pretty accurate representation of how our conditioning toward fear and self-hate keeps us from knowing our original nature.

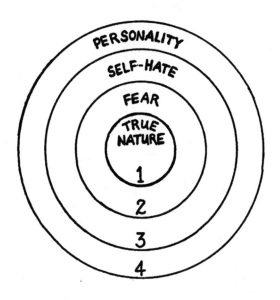

At the personality level (4), we have our coping mechanisms, all our defenses, our ways of getting by in the world. From this level, I might decide that I want something more than life is offering, that there must be something more to it than meets the eye.

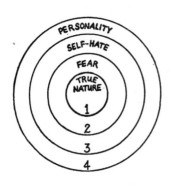

So I start working with the personality, trying to improve it, fix it, figure it out. I decide to get a different this or that, a new boyfriend/girlfriend, a new attitude, different friends, better grades. I pursue self-improvement, try really hard, make resolutions. I do all the things I think are going to turn me into the person I should be. There's nothing wrong with any of this, it just doesn't work.

Finally, all these efforts fail and I decide to take the Big Plunge and begin some kind of awareness process (such as reading this book!), maybe start a meditation practice, something that is designed to take me beyond the personality.

I begin the long, arduous journey to the center of my being. The first thing I run into is self-hate (3). Now this is the layer that, thankfully, has been keeping the personality level

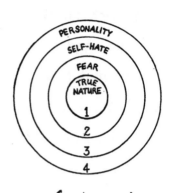

from working! We say "thankfully" because we are interested in awareness and ending suffering, not in being successful at becoming who self-hate says we must be.

So here I am at level 4 and I'm trying to become the perfect person, and level 3 is pointing out to me that it's not working. I'm going to improve myself and self-hate doesn't let me. Whenever I try to make a real beginning on this path of awareness, self-hate will do anything it can to stop me and then beat me for stopping.

I'm going to start being kind to myself and self-hate stops me and beats me for stopping. I'm going to start exercising and self-hate stops me and then beats me for stopping. I'm going to stop smoking and self-hate stops me from quitting and then beats me up for not quitting.

If I find the willingness to pay attention anyway,

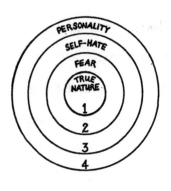

to struggle through all the self-hating voices, and I learn to hold on and pay attention to all of it and not be thrown off, the next level I encounter is fear (2).

I've made it past the distractions, I'm being kind to myself, and then there's this little moment of silence... What do I get? Fear. Big fear. It says, "You're going to die!" And I think, "How can that be the answer? I've gone through all this and FEAR IS THE ANSWER?"

So I come back to level 3, self-hate and I see that self-hate is pretty handy because it works in both directions: I can go from fear to self-hate, and I can go from personality to self-hate. It's flexible that way!

I can hate myself for being afraid and I can try to fix myself so that I'm not afraid and I can

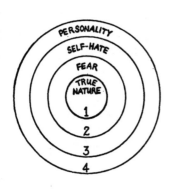

be afraid of the fear and I can hate myself for being afraid not to hate myself... all designed to stop me from getting to the center (1).

Perhaps, with patience and willingness and experience, or just plain old having suffered enough, I eventually realize that this whole process of going from personality to self-hate to fear to self-hate to personality and back again, has been exactly what I needed to be doing to learn what I needed to learn. I realize that every step I have taken has been on the Path.

Perhaps I realize that it has all been happening perfectly, and that True Nature was never inaccessible, never out of reach, always present, always guiding me. There never was anything wrong. I just didn't know it.

Horrible Things
(and I do mean horrible)

Self-hate is invested in convincing you that you are an awful person, that deep down inside you there is some Horrible Thing. Why? Because it stays in charge that way. It can just say

BOO!

and you'll jump back into line and do whatever it says. But you can call its bluff simply by saying, "BRING OUT THE HORRIBLE THING. SHOW IT TO ME."

Self-hate can't do that. And the more it cannot show you the Horrible Thing, the more it will dawn on you that

MAYBE IT DOESN'T EXIST. MAYBE THERE ISN'T A "HORRIBLE THING" INSIDE OF YOU.

Self-hate begins to scramble at this point because power is shifting away from it and shifting to

the part of you who is able to step back from self-hate and carry on this kind of dialogue with it,

the part of you that can begin to stop believing that there is something wrong with you

the part of you that is beginning to be free.

I maintain my identity
by not looking at myself.

This childhood system of survival, this belief in
"who I am", cannot hold up under scrutiny.
Nothing can.

So...
right before I begin to see myself (my
conditioned identity), the survival system goes on
the defensive and the voices start:
I'm bored.
This is stupid.
I don't need this.
I can't do this.
This doesn't work for me.
I've got too much to do.

It can sound as if we see self-hate as an enemy, but we don't. Gandhi talked about his political opponents as teachers, for to have worthy opponents is a blessing. They will force you to be the best that you are. That's the gift that self-hate is for us.

"I like the fact that I'm nice to just about everyone and that I can be the cheerful one in a tough situation, which really annoys some of my friends but also makes them feel better, which is all that matters. If I could change anything I would try to stop myself from talking about the people I don't like behind their backs. Even if I don't like them that doesn't give me the right to make fun of them on the phone with someone who also doesn't like them."

Regardless of what you were taught to believe, there <u>never</u> <u>was</u> anything wrong with you.

CHERI: Okay, let's hear some self-hate. Answer this: What is wrong with you?

GROUP: Everything . . . I can't figure out what is wrong . . . I can't get it right . . . I'm never serious . . . I'm ungrateful . . . I'm critical and judgmental . . . I'm hell-bound . . . I'm angry . . . I'm never going to get what I deserve . . . I'm not a team player . . . I'm a wimp . . . I'm closed . . . I can't be trusted . . . I'm a phony . . . I'm lazy and self-indulgent . . . I'm careless . . . I'm too serious . . . I'm a coward . . . I can't get with the program . . . I'm never satisfied . . . I don't pay attention . . . I talk too much . . . I'm too slow . . . I'm a quitter . . . I don't think enough . . . I can't keep up . . . I'm not good enough . . . I'm selfish . . . I'm mean . . . I'm unfriendly . . . I'm unworthy . . . I'm unlovable . . . I'm dishonest . . . I'm proud . . . I always have to be in control . . . I can't talk right . . .

I'm stupid . . . I'm out of control . . . I'm too emotional . . . I'm too sensitive . . .

CHERI: As you were answering, I watched people get littler and littler. You were taking a quick trip back to childhood. The voices changed, the body language changed, the energy changed. Suddenly, I was sitting in the room with a bunch of small children. These little children are very dear. And there is nothing wrong with them!

Conversation with Teens, continued

CH: What worked in the way you were raised?
--My parents gave me a lot of freedom, let me make choices, and just guided me.
--They let me be myself no matter how strange.
--They gave me strong roots. I have good morals.
--They taught me to do things like washing clothes, cooking, asking questions, and making appointments, just so I knew how.

CH: What didn't work in the way you were raised?
--They could have exposed me more to the real world and kept me more informed.
--They yelled too much.
--They could have trusted me more.
--They could have asked fewer questions and given me some space.
--They could have let me make more of my own choices.
--No hitting
--I wish they wouldn't fight in front of me.

--They punished me, but they didn't tell me I'm loved and appreciated.

--I wish they would involve me in the solution and leave the past behind us.

--I wish my parents hadn't pushed me so hard to do so many activities. As a child I played every sport and didn't understand half the rules.

To be continued...

Self-hate uses
SELF-IMPROVEMENT
as
SELF-MAINTENANCE.

As long as you are concerned about improving
yourself, you'll always have a false self to
improve. And you will always suffer.

It's No Wonder We Feel Inadequate

Self-hate encourages you to judge,
then it beats you for judging.

You judge someone else and it's simply self-hate
projected outward, then you get to use it back
on yourself when you beat yourself for judging!

We call this,
"Heads you lose,
tails you lose."

The Worst Thing That Could Happen

STUDENT: Belief in fairness is such a setup for self-hate. "If life were fair, if things were balanced the way they should be, this wouldn't be happening to me." It's easy to go from there to "I must have done something wrong." It's that old "why do bad things happen to good people?" I guess there aren't bad things and good people, just things and people.

CHERI: And that's frightening, isn't it? Because it means that we have no control. If anything can happen to us in spite of all our best efforts to make things go the way we want, where does that leave self-hate? One of self-hate's threats is, "If you don't do exactly as I say, something awful is going to happen to you."

If you believe this threat, the worst thing that can happen to you HAS ALREADY HAPPENED!

STUDENT: What is this "worst thing"?

161

CHERI: Believing that what the voices say about you is true. Believing that you are inadequate. Believing that you are not equal to your life. Turning away from your True Nature, your Heart, God.

"I wish we were seen in a more positive light. We are responsible people and we want to make a difference in the world."

IT IS REALLY QUITE MIRACULOUS, in the face
of all our conditioned fear, to be willing even to
consider just being with ourselves, and accepting
ourselves exactly as we are. We work and work
to uncover the layers of our conditioning, and
when we see what we've uncovered, our
reaction is,

"Oh, no, not that!
I don't want to see that."

What we did think we were going to see? We
must remember that this is the layer of "stuff"
between the one who is seeking and that which is
sought. It's what keeps me from ME. We have
been taught to hate it and fear it so that we'll
be too frightened and disgusted to look at it. It
knows that if we ever do
            if we ever get back
        to our unconditioned selves
            ☆ the jig is up! ☆
Getting back to who we really are means no
more illusion of separateness, no more self-
hate. That's why it's so hard and why almost no

one ever does it. Self-hate is very powerful and very clever and very determined, because it thinks it is fighting for its life.

So it looks worse and worse the deeper we go. That is why it's critical to learn to pay attention, to be aware, and believe nothing that the voices say to you. That's why it's so crucial to find compassion, to learn to trust yourself and be kind to yourself.

"In my ideal world there would be 1) love and respect for one another no matter what people looked like (love your neighbor as yourself and love yourself, too! 2) manners, and 3) yearning for learning what's best for themselves--a world free of alcohol, drugs, and explicit sex."

> "The voices tell me I'm fat, poor, ugly, have zits, not stylish, stupid, retarded."

> "The voices call me low-life, crap, know-nothing, waste of space, fat, ugly (inside and out), psycho, talentless, stupid, unlovable."

If the voice is not speaking compassionately, it has nothing worthwhile to tell you.*

*Everything you need to know will come to you in compassionate awareness.

Do not confuse
NICE & POLITE
with compassionate.

A compassionate person may be what we call nice and polite, but compassion does not try to be nice and polite.

Nice and polite come from conditioning.

Compassion comes from the Heart and our shared connectedness.

I had a teacher who said, after we did really poorly on a test, "I believe you people have the potential to be more in life than you have yet imagined." That stuck with me, and I did really well in that class.

Fake It 'Til You Make It

STUDENT: Much of my reluctance to do certain aspects of the work of ending self-hate comes from self-hate itself. For example, when I realize I am saying bad things to myself, it seems phony to make myself be compassionate by saying good things to myself instead. But I'm finding that just making the effort is often helpful. Recently I was been feeling crabby and not grateful, and just the mechanical act of writing 'thank you' was enough to help me find the sense of gratitude. I could say that was phony and stupid, but it worked.

CHERI: The voice saying it's phony is terrified that you'll find out how sincere you are.

STUDENT: It's okay to just pretend you like yourself, to go through the motions of embracing yourself, even if it feels false or stupid.

St. Theresa of Avila taught to go to the experience of gratitude within, and I've always assumed she meant fake it if it wasn't there. I often "act as if" and as soon as I do, I feel a real change.

CHERI: Because it's <u>not</u> phony. You are acting the way you really are, according to your True Nature, and that gets beneath the self-hate.

Stay with the Breath

STUDENT: I was at a class where we sat in meditation for an hour each morning. It was mentioned that if you hadn't sat before, you might have various physical sensations, even nausea. I had never meditated before, but I wanted to do everything right, so I sat every morning. Through every sitting I thought I was going to throw up. But since I knew to expect that kind of sensation, I kept sitting, and I made up my mind to stick it out even if I did throw up. What I learned was that I was able to get through it by staying with every single breath. And that experience showed me that the internal voices weren't right. They were saying, "You can't do this, you're going to be sick." But it wasn't true. Even the physical cues I was getting were false. That was an extremely valuable experience.

At another time in my life, when I was in a really difficult situation, it was true again that as long as I stayed with every breath and didn't believe the voices, I was all right. And that showed me where freedom is.

CHERI: Yes. If you went to another class and had a friend with you who was sitting for hours each day, even though he'd never sat before, you might say to him, "I hope you know what a great thing it is that you are doing."

   That's the kind of thing we'll say naturally to somebody we really care about, but we don't say to ourselves. But we could. We could even go beyond telling ourselves that it's okay to have our thoughts and feelings and risk something really compassionate like, "That was really good. I'm glad you did that. You're a good person." When I make those recommendations, people often say they're afraid that if they are that kind to themselves, they will become egocentric and self-indulgent. But we already are egocentric and self-indulgent! Being kind to ourselves is the way <u>not</u> to be egocentric and self-indulgent!

Conversation with Teens, continued

CH: Any advice for a friend who is struggling? What would you want to hear?

--Whatever it is, it can't be that bad.
--I'm here for you, if you need to talk, talk.
--I love you exactly the way you are.
--Just don't pay attention to what you don't want to be real.
--You can do it. Don't give up.

It's Okay to Feel Afraid?

STUDENT: I've found it very helpful in meditation to tell myself that I love myself. At first it felt sort of phony and ridiculous, but I decided to keep at it, and the results have been amazing. Sometimes I've been in really terrible mental states, and the idea of loving myself will come up all by itself. It's brought me to tears at times because the compassion is really there. I've practiced verbalizing "I love you" to myself, and as a result those words will just arise.

CHERI: The fact that we see it as "phony and ridiculous" tells us that self-hate is doing the judging. From a centered place, you would never see loving yourself as phony and ridiculous. Only ego would add those labels. Calling it phony is self-hate; it's ego trying to get you to believe that loving yourself is an experience that you don't know. That's why I like this process of reassuring myself that I do love myself.

An example of compassionate self-acceptance in action could be something like this: Let's say I've identified I'm afraid. I could say, "I am a brave and courageous person," but that's not going to do any good. Or I could say, "It's okay to be afraid," and begin to focus on what this fear is. "What is fear? What does it feel like? Where does it happen in my body? What do I say to myself when I'm afraid?" Then I may go ahead and do the thing I'm afraid of, and then I can ask, "At what point does the fear arise? How does the fear stop me from doing this thing? Can I feel the fear and do it anyway?" So, you see, there's somewhere to go with it. <u>If it's okay to be afraid</u>, all my options are open.

Am I afraid all the time? No. Well, when am I afraid? What exactly am I afraid of? If I'm trying to hide the fear, repress it, and not let myself know I have it, it can become a weapon for self-hate. Because instead of being someone who is afraid of a specific thing, I get labeled by self-hate as a frightened, fearful, whining, needy, cowardly person. But if I'm just afraid of something, <u>and</u> <u>that's</u> <u>okay</u>, that non-judgment is an open doorway through which I can go. The acceptance brings me back to myself. I can be with the fear as it's happening, experience it for what it is, and allow it to be healed within that acceptance.

"I used to feel absolutely safe in my ex-boyfriend's arms. Since we broke up three months ago, I don't have anywhere safe to go."

"When do I feel safe? When I'm in the car, late at night, cool air coming in the windows, music loud."

Fear is very dramatic.

It tells very plausible stories.

It makes strong feelings in your body.

It is the primary support of self-hate.

It is self-hate.

Self-hate is fear, and self-hate is everything it then does to manage, control and avoid that fear, that experience of itself. (It says, "I'll protect you. I'll keep you safe.")

Self-hate spends enormous amounts of time and energy pretending to avoid itself!

Pay attention.
Self-hate is slippery.
It will even say things to you like,

"You shouldn't believe the voices of self-hate.
If you are still believing them,

there really is something wrong with you!"

I am not here to become an acceptable person.

I am here to accept the person I am.

It May Be True...

It may be true that you make sacrifices, but that doesn't make you good, it just means you make sacrifices.

It may be true that you are accepting, but that doesn't make you good, it just means you are accepting.

It may be true that you are responsible, but that doesn't make you good, it just means you are responsible.

It may be true that you don't take drugs, but that doesn't make you good, it just means you don't take drugs.

It may be true that you don't have sex, but that doesn't make you good, it just means you don't have sex.

It may be true that you don't say mean things about people but that doesn't make you good, it just means you don't say mean things about people.

It may be true that you meditate, but that doesn't make you good, it just means you meditate.

We label these behaviors good and then continue to do them in order to support self-hate. Perhaps <u>doing</u> in order to be good is what keeps you from realizing that you are already good.

It may be true that you gossip, but that doesn't make you bad, it just means you gossip.

It may be true that you tell lies, but that doesn't make you bad, it just means you tell lies.

It may be true that you are impatient, but that doesn't make you bad, it just means you are impatient.

It may be true that you cheat in school but that doesn't make you bad, it just means you cheat.

It may be true that you steal but that doesn't make you bad, it just means you steal.

It may be true that you take drugs but that doesn't make you bad, it just means you take drugs.

It may be true that you are sarcastic, but that doesn't make you bad, it just means you are sarcastic.

We label these behaviors bad and then continue to do them in order to support self-hate. Believing that what you do determines who you are could be the real reason for continuing the behaviors.

It's a lose/lose game with self-hate.

If I feel good
I have to pay the price
because it's not really okay to feel good.

If I feel bad
I have to pay the price
because it's not really okay to feel bad.

But I Could Make A Mistake!

STUDENT: I've heard you say that it's not possible to make mistakes. I'm having some difficulty understanding this. Would you say more about it?

CHERI: Whatever it is that I'm doing, if I pay attention to it, I'm going to benefit. I'm going to learn something.

Look at a child learning to walk. At what point should she consider herself a failure and give up? All of the times she pitches over on her head or falls back on her bottom? Those are not successful from the definition of walking, yet they are not unsuccessful, either. They are just part of the process of learning to walk.

If we want to wake up and end our suffering (and if we are paying attention to how we cause ourselves to suffer), we are going to learn from everything that happens. For example, I am going along in life working diligently toward something, and it doesn't go the way I want it to go. If I am willing to pay attention, not getting what I want is very helpful.

"Why didn't I get what I wanted?"

"Why wasn't I in control?"

"What went wrong?"

"Who's to blame?"

"What should I have done differently?"

"Maybe I should try harder."

Well, now, <u>there's</u> a classroom for you!

If you were to see clearly all your conditioned beliefs about getting what you want, about control, wrong, blame, should, and trying, you would have a level of clarity that would make your life simple and enjoyable in a way that you cannot now even imagine. You would have a level of freedom available to you that you would never find if everything went the way you want it to for the rest of your life.

If you are afraid of making a mistake, you've already made it. You're already in as bad a place as you can be in. Everything after that is getting out.

This kind of information is not well received by self-hate because what would it beat you with if it weren't possible to fail? If there were no such thing as a mistake? If you couldn't do it wrong? And if there were nothing to beat you with, how could it maintain control over you? What would maintain the fear? What would maintain the anxiety and the inadequacy?

It is only the illusion of a separate self (something that believes itself to be outside of life and living in other than the Now, which is the only reality) who could believe it is possible to make mistakes. Because, in fact, there isn't anything going on other than what is. It is only in some imaginary parallel universe in which this is what did happen but something else could have happened, that that kind of alternative seems plausible. In this universe there is only what is. Everything else is imagination.

As far as I know, it is only when we hold the notion that something happened <u>this</u> way, but it should have happened <u>that</u> way that we can say, "Well, I had <u>this</u> experience, but <u>that</u> is the one I was supposed to have." I don't think so.

STUDENT: From the perspective of the part of me who believes in failure, none of what you're saying makes sense, and yet, what you're saying makes sense.

CHERI: That's why, when we look at these issues, it is very helpful to come back to center, the present moment, to look at them because self-hate is <u>invested</u> <u>in</u> <u>failure</u>.

The payoff for failing?
AS LONG AS YOU FAIL,
YOU GET TO KEEP TRYING.

So you have to do it again. "I don't have it quite right so I have to do it again."

STUDENT: How could that be a payoff?

CHERI: It maintains my sense of who I am, my place at the center of the universe. The whole universe is hinged on "Will I make it?" And I will say again what I have said so often. The reason acceptance, simply accepting what is, is not more popular is that in acceptance, there is nothing <u>to do</u>. "Who I am" <u>is</u> doing, doing something to be different, to be other than what is.

And remember,
self-hate,
egocentricity,
fear,
misery,
the illusion of separation,
is ultimately concerned with only one thing:

maintaining itself.

I suspect we focus on "learning from our mistakes" (beating ourselves up over them) because that keeps us from paying attention to what we are doing

NOW.

Remember,
as long as you are out of the moment,
self-hate is in control.

Nonacceptance
is always
suffering,
no matter
what you're
not accepting.

Acceptance
is always
freedom,
no matter
what you're
accepting.

A Definition of Suffering

Trying to get and hold on
to that which we like,

and

trying to avoid and eliminate
that which we do not like.

Whatever is struggling
or discontent
or suffering
or afraid

__is__ that which needs to be accepted.

Self-Hate and the Illusion of Control

Life is very short. We do not have time to be frightened. We do not have the luxury of allowing fear and hate to run our lives.

THIS IS IT!

We're tense and stress-filled, trying to control life. We tense up, hold on tightly, and feel that we're making something happen (what we want), or keeping something from happening (what we don't want). If, in fact, by tensing up we could control life, we'd be foolish not to. However, we know that being tense and filled with stress does <u>not</u> enable us to control life.

Aren't we then quite foolish
to maintain the tension?

Because with this tense-but-no-control situation, we have two problems:

1. tension/stress and
2. no control over life.

In a no-tension-but-no-control situation, we would have only one problem:

1. no control over life

which can be experienced as
frightening
or
freedom.

We have no control
but we think we __should__ have.

Letting go of the illusion of control
            will not make you more vulnerable,
it will make you more
open,
  calm,
    joyful,
      relaxed,
        peaceful,
          receptive.

Children have no control and don't think
they should have.

"Yes, but look what happens to kids!"

Life is life with or without the illusion of
control. Children feel the pain of life, of course.
But, pain and suffering are not the same thing.

Suffering happens
when we are taught to believe
that what is happening to us is
wrong
and
a mistake,

and
we should have
prevented it!

We <u>learn</u> to think of life as reward and punishment.

- If I'm good, good things happen to me. I get what I want. ("Eat your peas then you can have pie.")

- If I'm bad, bad things happen to me. I won't get what I want, and things will be withheld from me. ("You didn't do your homework. No television for you tonight.")

We learn to believe that
if we exert enough control,
if we are how we "should" be,
we can have only the good things in
life and keep anything "bad" from
happening to us.

We learn to believe that
what happens to us
is the result of how we are.

We learn to believe that
life rewards us when we're good
and punishes us when we're bad.

Before long we are firmly entrenched in "Things are going my way. That means I'm a good person." Or "I'm not getting what I want. I'm being punished for being bad."

This is what's going on in a nutshell: We have learned to believe that self-hate--that relentless onslaught of judgment, criticism, and blame--is what prevents us from being cruel, exploitative, selfish, and indulgent, and that without being constantly watched and controlled we will be hateful and harmful.

"I wish my parents had sat down and talked with me. I'm going to sit down and talk with my kids instead of hitting them."

Self-hate won't prevent
the abuse of little children
who are currently in little bodies,
and it won't prevent the abuse
of little children who are currently
in big bodies (such as your own).

The only way
we are ever going to stop abuse
in all its forms
is by ceasing to believe
that punishing people
makes them good.

You cannot be nonviolent
if there is any part of you
that you are in opposition to.

You are not truly giving
if there is any part of
yourself to which you will not
extend compassion.

Your love will always be conditional
as long as you are excluding
any part of yourself from it.

Suffering cannot be healed through self-hate. Only through compassionate acceptance can suffering be healed.

If we accept, if we open ourselves, life will transform us. If we resist, if we try to run away, the conditioning that causes us to suffer deepens.

When we embrace, when we accept, the pain wears the suffering away.

If we can be willing and patient, life will work its magic on us. Little by little, all that is not compassion will be stripped away, burned away, from us. The pain and suffering of holding on to our beliefs and fears will become so great that we will let go. And each time we let go, we find peace, relief, ease, and a growing sense of gratitude and compassion.

Meditation Will Take Care of It

STUDENT: I wake up in the night afraid of dying. I don't know what to do.

CHERI: Meditating will take care of it for you. You will be able to experience directly what you are labeling fear. What is fear actually? "Well, I'm afraid I'm going to die." You are going to die, that's true. Are you dying in this moment? Not so that it shows. Is it an <u>experience</u> you're having, or is it an <u>idea</u> you're holding onto? What would that sensation be without those beliefs, without those labels, without that conditioning?

You wake up, and everything is fine. A thought goes through your head, fear follows it, more voices kick in, and you're off to the races. There was nothing going on before that. How did you get there? What happened?

STUDENT: There were times when I would stay awake all night.

CHERI: Believing every bit of what the voices in your head were saying, right? So, you begin to see how that kind of process has served a purpose in your life. Now, the purpose may be no more complex than it perpetuates self-hate. It keeps you down. It keeps you terrified. It keeps you stuck. It keeps you "safe." You start to take a risk, you feel the icy hand around the spine at 3:00 A.M., you knock off that risk-taking. ("Okay, okay I'll be the person I should be, just don't let me die!") You just high-tail it back to that safe place. Start doing all of those behaviors that make your survival system feel in control and feel safe. Narrow the world down. Do what you're supposed to do. Beat yourself mercilessly, and then maybe you'll be all right.

Through a practice of paying attention as closely as you can, you will begin to suspect that what's really going on is a process that has nothing to do with what you think is going on. You begin to see that there are certain times when these patterns happen. You begin to notice that they are, in fact, patterns. You're no longer believing them. You're bringing it back closer and closer to the sensation that's actually triggering it. And you realize that there is no such thing as fear.

🧘

"I don't feel similar to many of my peers because I feel I am on a different intellectual level than most. In other words, I'm not brain dead. A lot of teenagers think adults are too hard on them, but in defense of the adults, most teenagers don't use their heads."

Beginning to wake up.
Starting to see through the fog of
confusion that childhood social
conditioning has left us in.

Beginning not to take it personally.
Beginning to see that life isn't
anyone's "fault."

It just is
and you just are
and it's all just fine.

A Solid Program for Ending Suffering

CHERI: To me, the psychological work we do is wonderfully helpful, but it's useless without learning to pay close attention, and the fastest way to do that is meditation. Now, meditation practice is not useless without the psychological aspect. You could just sit down and face a blank, white wall and eventually you would understand everything about how life works. It's all available without having any intellectual understanding of it. However, the two together are a really solid program for ending suffering. It is true most people want to have only an intellectual understanding and then make that work for them. But it's like having an intellectual understanding of riding a bicycle. It's great when you're sitting in the living room with a book reading about it, but when you are flying down a hill, it doesn't help. The only thing that's helpful is doing it, participating, practicing.

In our meditation practice, we go to a place of inherent goodness, we find a deep sense of well-being within ourselves, and we become friends with that. We go there, and we see that being there is wonderful. For the periods of time that we're there, all the problems fall away, everything falls into place. And then we leave that well-being and go get caught up in something. And we come back. That's why I talk about, rather than taking our awareness practice into daily life, we bring our daily life into our awareness practice. We're creating a circle of compassion, and we keep bringing the events of our life into it. If I am troubled and upset about something, I bring it into that still place, and there's peace there. It just resolves itself. It dissolves. Then I get caught up again, my mind takes off, I go into the conditioning, and I'm miserable again. Then I come back. I practice coming back here (indicating center), going out, getting miserable, coming back here. Eventually I get to the point where when I look at being here in the place of compassion, or being out there caught up in self-hate, there's just no question about it. I don't want to be out there caught up in self-hate. It's not that I'm pushing that away; it's not that I'm saying I'm a bad person for doing that. It's just that I look at it, I realize what's going on, I want to come back here.

Who's Afraid of Me? I'm Afraid of Me!

The benefit of working to let go of self-hate is that you cease to be afraid of yourself, and find a greater willingness to accept whatever is there inside you. When you stop believing the voices of self-hate, you will notice a curious thing: emptiness, a hole inside yourself. Instead of distracting yourself and trying to fill it up, if you become curious about how to be <u>with</u> the emptiness, it is a very wonderful thing.

When we try to fill up that hole with distractions, we are left feeling alone, isolated, abandoned, empty. When we allow the emptiness to be what it is, we find it to be an open, spacious feeling. (This makes ego uncomfortable because it doesn't exist there!) So, getting used to that spaciousness is a wonderful experience. That emptiness is all potential, every possibility. It is who we truly are.

In the present,
we can embrace the past
and free the future.

If the future is not freed
to be the present it is,
our present will always
be lived in the past.

All of life's conflicts are between
letting go
or
holding on

opening into the present
or
clinging to the past

expansion
or
contraction.

Acceptance is the path to creativity,
in fact,
it _is_ creativity.

Until you accept, nothing new can be.
You will have only the past.

If you want a new world,
accept the world as it is.

If you want a wholly new world,
accept it wholly.

SAY

YES

TO LIFE

When the Buddha wanted to find out how suffering happened and how to end it, and discovered that no one could tell him, his response was to find out for himself.

It is possible for each of us to do this. Each of us has the ability to find out for ourselves everything we want to know. We can end our suffering.

Almost Nobody Wants to Grow Up.

We think it's too hard. We would rather focus on what's wrong with us and why we can't do anything about it.

We don't want <u>to take care of ourselves</u> because that means giving up the wish <u>to be taken care of by someone else</u>.

"I want my mother to do it. She should have done it but she didn't. I'm going to stay stuck right here until ..."

Until what? Until she does it? But she can't do it. And she never could.

Again, we need to consider this: If we can't take care of ourselves now, how could somebody else have done it? "Well I could do it now if she had done it then."

No.

That's a scam run by self-hate designed to keep you stuck.

We look for things that were done to us because that makes us The Victim. When we are The Victim, things are not our fault, and we don't have to take responsibility. We can point to all these reasons that we are how we are.

We can also say, yes, this did happen to me, and my parents did it to me because their parents did it to them, and so on down the line. And if I can't stop doing it to myself, how can I expect them to have stopped doing it? They weren't aware any of this existed. They were just trying to be good parents in the only way they knew to parent--the way they were parented. When we really understand this, we have great sympathy for the fact that our parents were never given the love and acceptance they so desperately needed as children.

ALMOST NOBODY WANTS TO GROW UP.

Taking responsibility
is not
taking blame.

It's not your fault.
It's not someone else's fault.
It's not anyone's fault.

"FAULT" MISSES THE POINT.

This is how it is.
This is your best opportunity to turn it around.*

*There will always be future opportunities, but why not use this one?

- paraphrase of an old Zen story -

One hot summer afternoon, the monastery cook, an elderly monk, was spreading mushrooms on a mat to dry in the sun. A young monk saw him and asked, "Why is an old man like you doing such hard work in the heat of the day?" The old monk replied, "If not me, who? If not now, when?"

- paraphrase of another old Zen story -

A woman went to a Zen monastery. She was so thrilled to be there--such a holy place, a place of enlightenment. The first meditation period, she walked mindfully up the steps of the meditation hall. As she was preparing to bow deeply before entering, she noticed a shocking thing. There, at the top of the steps, was a bucket of filthy wash water with a mop protruding from the murky depths. "That's awful!" she exclaimed, truly horrified, and went in to meditate. The next morning the bucket was still there. "That's disgusting," she muttered, "this is Zen?" and went in to meditate. The next morning, the same bucket. She exclaimed, "I can't believe this! This is ridiculous. Someone should do something about this," and went in to meditate The fourth morning, there was the bucket, hardly improved by the days of neglect. The woman looked at the bucket and thought, "I'm someone," and took it away and cleaned it.

It doesn't matter how young or old we are, it is up to each of us to take a step right now--one moment, one breath, one choice, one word-- toward being the way we want the world to be.

If you want people to be kind, be kind.
If you want people to be trustworthy, be trustworthy.
If you want people to listen to you, listen to them. (You can't make someone be a good listener, but you can model being a good listener.)
If you want people to talk to you, talk to them. (You can't make someone be a good communicator, but you can model being a good communicator.)

People 40, 50, 60 years old are waiting for their parents to parent them. "I don't want to have to love myself. I want my mother to love me. I want my father to give me what I need." The odds are very good that that's not going to happen.

If your parents could love you
the way you want to be loved,
it already would have happened.

Here is a notion: You could love your parents (and yourself and every one else you come in contact with) the way you want to be loved, the way you wish your parents had loved you.

Only you
know how you want and need to be loved.

Only you
can love you the way you want and need to be
loved.

If you can't or won't give yourself what you
need, how do you suppose <u>someone else</u>,
who isn't nearly so motivated,
who, in fact, is looking to get it for themselves
(possibly from you!)
is going to provide it for you?

ALMOST NOBODY WANTS TO GROW UP.

We Can Have It All

Living from compassion for ourselves
gives us each
the loving parent
we've always wanted.

CHERI: I used to think I was going to find within myself a grownup to parent my child. I've discovered that it's really a case of finding the child who can care for the grownup! The secret is this. The adult is the abused product of society's conditioning, while the child, who was (thank goodness) abandoned so that this person could survive, is still here inside, whole and complete and original.

What we are doing in awareness practice is experiencing that who we <u>are</u> is not the self-hating social conditioning. Who we <u>are</u> is the conscious, compassionate awareness that is our essential nature. As we learn to live more from essence, we grow to realize that it is our opportunity, our joy, and our delight to embrace into unconditional love and acceptance everyone and everything that suffers.

You have to take responsibility for living TODAY the life you want to live.

WHAT I WANT IN MY LIFE	CHECK(✓) ONE		
	YES	NO	MAYBE
ACCEPTANCE			
REJECTION			
COMPASSION			
JUDGMENT			
CLARITY			
SHOULDS			
FREEDOM			
RESISTANCE			
MASTERY			
OTHER			

The only difference between the life you are living and the life you want to live is the feeling of being appreciated, loved and accepted. Unconditionally.

So ...

GIVE IT TO YOURSELF!
RIGHT NOW!
THIS MINUTE!
DON'T WAIT!

Not when you've changed. Not when you're in a better mood. Not when you've earned it. RIGHT NOW! You could start with appreciating yourself for reading this book, for caring, for being willing, for opening your heart.

Stop for just a moment, take a long deep breath, and tell yourself three things you like best about yourself.

There is nothing in life
that could happen to you
that is worse than living in fear and self-hate.

And the great sadness
is that living in fear and self-hate
won't keep what you fear and hate
from happening to you.

I can twist myself into a knot, beat and punish myself into appearing to be the way I think people want me to be, and they <u>still</u> might not like me. If I am me, a person I like and respect, at least I can be sure one person will like me... ME!

A hint: A person who likes himself tends to be liked by most everybody. Why? Because when we feel liked and appreciated, we're happy and happy people tend to be well-liked.

We cling to our belief that there is something wrong

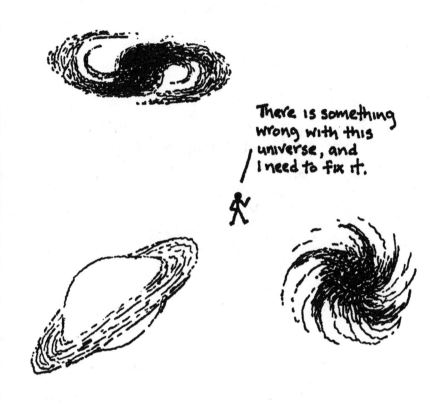

There is something wrong with this universe, and I need to fix it.

because that's how we maintain our position at the center of the universe.

The best reason to look at self-hate is that it gets in the way of being able to live the full, happy life that is your potential.

It gets in the way of finding that place of deep compassion within ourselves that is the largest part of a joyful, successful life.

It doesn't matter what happened

THEN.

It only matters what happens

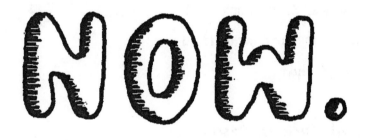

If you stop worrying about what happened THEN (the past) you can live in infinite possibility NOW (the present).

We Have A Choice.

We can live our lives trying to conform to some
nebulous standard,
or
we can live our lives seeing how everything
works.

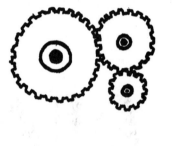

When we step back and
look at it that way, it is
obvious that

the attitude of fascination
is the only intelligent one to bring to anything.

Compassion, No Matter What

CHERI: There's nothing more important in life than compassion. Anything other than compassion is designed to pull us off center. Everything other than compassion is self-hate. Don't fall for it. You can embrace every part of life in compassion, just like you would accept and embrace a mischievous friend.

If there is judgment, it is coming from self-hate. From center, from compassion, there is no judgment. There is no element of wrong or bad. So you don't have to be fooled any longer. Self-hate will be the one who's saying, "Well, yeah, but that isn't a <u>judgment</u>. That's just clarity of perception. I'm actually centered and I can see that from a centered place, you really are a bad person." WRONG.

STUDENT: It is helpful to have an external person saying, "Do you see how you're looking from self-hate here?" Is the idea eventually to have that kind of perspective internally?

CHERI: Absolutely. What you're learning to do through this work is to see yourself from compassionate awareness. When you're seeing from compassionate awareness you can see everything clearly. You're finding that place inside of you, and you move in and out of it, right? And eventually that will become your, this has to be in quotes, "identity." You will simply live from that place. You will be pulled off occasionally into self-hate, but you will live from compassionate awareness.

"With my own children, I will teach them to accept people for who they are. I will try to teach them to make right choices and let them experience the consequences of a "wrong" choice. I will be a shoulder to cry on. I will help them to be independent, self-sufficient, and understanding as well as having their own points of view."

When you simply watch
the next movement
of the mind,

I should...

and the next,

I need to...

and the next,

I can't...

the whole mass of conditioning
you've been taught to believe
begins
        to
           fall
                away...

Miracles

It is a miracle:

- to be someone who has seen a different possibility

- to want to wake up and end suffering

- to pay attention and see how you've been conditioned to believe

- to get your head above water (or out of the stew pot) for any length of time

- to have even a glimmering of how it all works

- to have the willingness to do this work at all.

Jesus said,

"You must become as little children."

He was talking about having as our primary identity the innocent Heart, not the conditioned mind. From the innocent, compassionate Heart it is clear that life just happens. We don't need to take it personally. We are not being punished, and neither are we being rewarded. It is only when we are identified with our socialized, conditioned minds that we have difficulty with any of it.

You have to have faith that
in this moment,
in each moment,
you,
exactly as you are,
are perfectly adequate
and equal to your life.

Some Tools and Techniques

Learning to pay attention and see through self-hate by yourself is difficult, but certainly not impossible. If you have a friend, counselor, or teacher who understands this work, or would be willing to learn about it, that person can assist you in keeping the perspective of disidentification that self-hate will be diligently attempting to remove from you. You might consider passing this book along to any person whom you would like to assist you in keeping this new, no-more-self-hate perspective. Remember that maintaining itself is the primary focus of self-hate. It is clever, slippery, and tricky. In the beginning, it will fool you more often than not. And that's okay. This is not a contest. What you're learning in this work is to have compassion for yourself no matter what.

Keeping that firmly in the front of your awareness, here are some suggestions to get you started:

Ask yourself what are the things you've always wanted someone to say to you, but no one ever has.

Ask the child inside you what he needs to hear you say.

Make a tape. RECORD the things you've always wanted someone else to say. Include everything the child needs to hear to feel loved.

Listen to the tape every day. Add to it when you think of something else you want to hear.

Write letters of appreciation to yourself.

Think of at least one kind thing to do for yourself each day.

Make a list of things you'd like to have and begin providing them for yourself.

Each time you give a gift to someone else, give something (even if it's just little) to yourself.

Stop and appreciate yourself for every thought and act of kindness.

Say thank you to yourself when you do something kind.

Each time you receive a gift, give something (even if it's just something little!) to someone else, and really let yourself feel the joy of doing it.

Get comfortable saying, "I love you" to yourself and say it many times each day.

Take out pictures of yourself when you were little, frame them, place them in prominent places, and let yourself begin to appreciate that little person.

Journal regularly, noting the self-hating ways you speak to yourself and treat yourself. When you become aware of a self-hating thought or action, write it down and remind yourself that even though you were taught to treat yourself that way, you are now committed to unconditional love and acceptance for yourself.

And, of course, we would encourage a time of quiet and solitude each day (preferable a time of meditation) in order to be more present to yourself.

"I have grown up in the foster care system and have had over 20 sets of guardians/parents. One of the things I remember that worked was when one set of foster parents would tell me what I needed to work on for the next day. That was a huge help. When I went to bed I thought about how I wanted the next day to be and even though I usually ended up making mistakes, it helped me to have a direction."

Compassionate Communication

As you begin this work, you may find that you're going to have to take responsibility for getting folks around you (like parents) to join you in the work. Uncomfortable as it might be, you might need to be the one initiating, and keeping alive, the process of ending self-hate in your world. As suggested earlier, one of the simplest ways of getting started is by asking your family, teachers, minister, coach, and other significant adults, as well as your friends, to read this book. In that way you will all be speaking the same language.

You may need to ask adults in your life for commitments about communication.
For instance:
--Can we agree to listen to each other without arguing?
--Can we each have three minutes to say what is so for us?

--Can we get an unbiased third-party to facilitate our communication?
--Would you be willing to practice some communication skills with me?

Here are some techniques that can facilitate ending self-hating communication:

--Make "I" statements, avoid "you" statements.
   Rather than saying "You..." practice speaking about your own experience beginning with "I...." Thus, "You never listen to what I'm saying," becomes, "I don't feel heard." In this way each person takes responsibility for their own experience rather than projecting it onto the other.

--Avoid "why" questions.
   Why questions tend to take us up into our heads (the land of social conditioning) rather than getting us the information we're looking for. Thus, "Why do you want to do that?" becomes, "Will you tell me about wanting to do that?" This

actually produces the information we want to have.

--Avoid "always" and "never."

Generalizing and globalizing takes us away from the subject at hand and leads us into a world of accusation and alienation. Thus, "You always do what you want. You never think about what I want," becomes, "I don't feel considered in the plans you've made."

--Use "and" instead of "but."

"But" tends to negate everything that comes before it in a sentence. "I really want to go with you, but I have a test tomorrow." The real information comes after the "but." If both things are equally important pieces of information, using "and" communicates the equality. "I really want to go with you, AND I have a test tomorrow." Often the information before the "but" is just there to soften the blow of the real information. This technique helps you say what you mean.

--Use "When you____, I feel____."

Again, we're attempting to take the accusation out of our communication. Thus, "You are so selfish," becomes "When you leave without telling me, I feel not valued." It can be helpful to add something such as, "and that gets in the way of my ability to be open and loving with you."

--Practice reflective listening, drawing out, and clarifying

Reflective or "active" listening, really paying attention to what someone is saying to us, is one of the great gifts we can give and receive in relationship. When you speak I listen, take in what you say, and say it back to you exactly as you've said it. I don't interpret, correct, or amend. I hear exactly what you have said. This gives both of us our best chance to hear what you have to say. (Often we don't actually listen to ourselves!)

I can ask you questions such as, "Did I get that right?" or "Is there more?" to help you to continue to communicate and to help me to continue to listen. When we're both sure we have heard and understood what you have to say, we can hear what I have to say. Back and forth, until we are each complete with the communication.

> I often feel angry and frustrated. They don't listen or care about my feelings. It's always, "NO," and when I ask why they say, "I don't need to give you a reason."

Here are some fill-in-the-blanks that may assist in a growing understanding between teens and parents:

Please tell me what you mean by _____.
For instance:
"a bad influence"
"leads to trouble"
"will ruin your life"

I don't understand the importance of

_____.

For instance:

  going to college

  cleaning my room

Please tell me why you don't want me to

_____.

For instance:

  talk on the phone

  hang out with my friends

What is it about _____ that upsets you?

For instance:

  kids my age having sex

  me making mistakes

  having my own opinion

Is it true that adults don't want teenagers to

_____.

For instance:

  have fun

  think for themselves

What do adults mean by _____.
For instance:
   "You (me, teenager) just don't understand."
   "Because I said so," or "Because I'm the
parent."

These kinds of questions are so "charged" for
adults that it might be helpful to take the book
with you to the conversation. Point out where
the question you want to ask fits in, and then
use the language in the book to ask your
question. This will show the adult that you are
actually seeking information, not just "mouthing
off," or "talking back." Remember adults are
heavily conditioned, too. We need time to adjust
to new ways of doing things. Be patient.

These processes can seem awkward and forced
until we get used to them. However, they only
feel awkward and forced because we're so
conditioned to communicate unconsciously and
unkindly. This new type of interaction is based
on the premise that both parties are good

people with good intentions who wish to get along as well as possible. Despite appearances, parents and teens do not wish to be enemies. Both sides tend to see themselves as trying hard and being misunderstood. Using these communication techniques can make the trying hard pay off and decrease dramatically the incidents of misunderstanding.

It is true that this type of communication is time consuming, however, if we consider the amount of time it takes to act out, get in trouble, fight, pout, appease, reconcile, ignore, insult, and retaliate, clear communication becomes a real time-saver.

Another suggestion: practice assuming the best. Most of us have learned to assume the worst, which does not lead us to the open, honest, loving relationships we wish to have in our families. What does that look like? When someone asks, "Why?" assume they really want to know. Assume they don't know and are sincerely asking for information. Their technique may be unskilled, but that doesn't mean they're being hateful, sarcastic, or judgmental. If we are going to assume anything about our loved ones, let's assume that they are good people who love us and then proceed from that perspective.

The only way out of this life of suffering is through the doorway of compassion.

"But how do I find the doorway?"

You can't <u>find</u> it because you <u>are</u> it. The moment there is nothing left of you but compassion, you ARE the doorway.

The door is wide open and you are free.

We have *There Is Nothing Wrong With You* retreats designed especially for teens. We also have retreats for parents. Please contact us if you would like more information on a retreat.

Zen Monastery Practice Center
P.O. Box 1979
Murphys, CA 95247

Telephone: 209-728-0860

Fax: 209-728-0861

Email: zencentr@volcano.net

Website: www.thezencenter.org

For a one-year subscription to the Center's quarterly newsletter and calendar of events, *In Our Practice*, send a check for $12.00 along with your name and address.

To order books by American Zen teacher
Cheri Huber

Available from your local bookstore or order in the following ways:
Call toll-free 1-800-337-3040. Fax order to 1-209-728-0861.
To order by mail, send order and payment to the address below.
Visa, Mastercard and Discover card accepted.

____	There Is Nothing Wrong With You Revised Edition*	0-9710309-0-1	$12.00
____	There Is Nothing Wrong With You for TEENS*	0-9636255-9-4	$12.00
____	How You Do Anything Is How You Do Everything: A Workbook	0-9636255-5-1	$10.00
____	The Depression Book*	0-9636255-6-X	$12.00
____	The Fear Book*	0-9636255-1-9	$10.00
____	Be the Person You Want to Find*	0-9636255-2-7	$12.00
____	The Key and the Name of the Key Is Willingness*	0-9636255-4-3	$10.00
____	Nothing Happens Next	0-9636255-3-5	$8.00
____	Sex and Money: A Guided Journal	0-9636255-7-9	$12.00
____	Suffering Is Optional	0-9636255-8-6	$12.00
____	That Which You Are Seeking Is Causing You To Seek*	0-9614754-6-3	$10.00
____	Time-Out for Parents*	0-9614754-4-7	$12.00

*Also available as a book on tape. Call for prices.
Books and tapes are sold in discounted sets. Call for prices and a catalog.

Name: _____

Address _____

City _____ State _____ Zip _____

Please send the books I have checked above $ _____

Postage and Handling: $3 each book, $1 for each add'l book $ _____

7.25% Sales Tax (California residents only) $ _____

TOTAL ENCLOSED $ _____

If ordering by mail and using a credit card, send card number and expiration
date to: **KEEP IT SIMPLE, P.O. BOX 1979, MURPHYS, CA 95247**
Orders out of U.S. send double postage. Overpayments will be refunded. A
complete catalog will be sent with your order.